ANXIETY TO EMPOWERMENT

EXERCISES & MEDITATIONS TO
STOP STRESSING &
START ENGAGING

Llewellyn Publications

Woodbury, Minnesota

AMANDA HUGGINS

FIRST EDITION
First Printing, 2024

Book design by Samantha Peterson
Cover design by Shannon McKuhen
Interior illustrations by Llewellyn Art Department

Photography is used for illustrative purposes only. The persons depicted may not endorse or represent the book's subject.

Llewellyn Publications is a registered trademark of Llewellyn Worldwide Ltd.

Library of Congress Cataloging-in-Publication Data
Names: Huggins, Amanda (Anxiety and mindfulness coach), author.
Title: Anxiety to empowerment : exercises & meditations to stop stressing & start engaging / by Amanda Huggins.
Description: First edition. | Woodbury, MN : Llewellyn Publications, [2024] | Includes bibliographical references. | Summary: "This comprehensive guide enables you to fully understand your own patterns, break free of harmful cycles, and transform your stress into clear boundaries, healing, and success" —Provided by publisher.
Identifiers: LCCN 2024001979 (print) | LCCN 2024001980 (ebook) | ISBN 9780738774947 (paperback) | ISBN 9780738775081 (ebook)
Subjects: LCSH: Anxiety. | Stress (Psychology) | Meditation—Therapeutic use.
Classification: LCC BF575.A6 H84 2024 (print) | LCC BF575.A6 (ebook) | DDC 152.4/6—dc23/eng/20240205
LC record available at https://lccn.loc.gov/2024001979
LC ebook record available at https://lccn.loc.gov/2024001980

Llewellyn Worldwide Ltd. does not participate in, endorse, or have any authority or responsibility concerning private business transactions between our authors and the public.

All mail addressed to the author is forwarded but the publisher cannot, unless specifically instructed by the author, give out an address or phone number.

Any internet references contained in this work are current at publication time, but the publisher cannot guarantee that a specific location will continue to be maintained. Please refer to the publisher's website for links to authors' websites and other sources.

Llewellyn Publications
A Division of Llewellyn Worldwide Ltd.
2143 Wooddale Drive
Woodbury, MN 55125-2989
www.llewellyn.com

Printed in the United States of America

Praise for *Anxiety to Empowerment*

"I've come to know Amanda's work independently and am in incredible awe of her integrative approach—body, mind, and soul….She has keen insights, structure, process, and genuine compassion."

—CYNDI DALE, internationally renowned author of thirty bestselling books, including *Energy Healing for Trauma, Stress & Chronic Illness*

"Amanda Huggins is a force and a gift. She has the unique and keen ability to translate incredibly heady information into easily digestible bites without diminishing the power and potency of the message."

—MELANIE C. KLEIN, high-level empowerment coach and professor of sociology and gender/women's studies

"Amanda blends many of the most effective tenants of traditional therapy with the dynamic and spiritual elements of Universal Law….This combination is a breath of fresh air for anyone looking for a better, more holistic approach to mental health."

—MICHAEL GRILLO, head of consumer products at Calm software company and cofounder of Gravity Blankets

"Amanda showed me how to reset my life by becoming more self-aware in the present moment."

—SEAN FAGAN, owner of Impact Fitness gyms

"Amanda is a fantastic teacher and coach who puts everything into a real-life context, making it easy to understand."

—NICOLE LEVINGS, global brand director at Agency TK

"The tools Amanda gave me opened up the door for me to accept that I have worth, I have gifts, and I have permission to explore the stories my anxiety tells me."

—KARLA DEL ANGEL, freelance digital marketing director

"Amanda helped me do the real work I needed to do to understand my anxious thoughts and showed me the tools to manage them in my everyday interactions."

—ABBY COHN, vice president of brand and communications at SK Group

"Amanda honors her duality as a coach whose responsibility is to keep you accountable and as a friend who will sit with you as you navigate some of the hardest and darkest parts of yourself."

—NEEYAZ ZOLFAGHARI, founder of Unspoken Nutrition

"Amanda is transforming the conversations around anxiety and mental health....Her loving, spiritual, and tactical approach is changing the coaching world."

—LISA BATTAGLIA, founder and host of *The Elevated Podcast*

"Amanda helped me with both immediate exercises to triage daily anxiety and steps to plan for long-term fulfillment."

—DAVID WORHMAN, senior program manager at Amazon

"Amanda…has created a unique approach to not just understanding and contextualizing anxiety, but also provides clear steps to seniority in the space of anxiety through tools, techniques, and meditations."

—CYNDI MAUER, host of *Into the Known* podcast

"Amanda really helped me identify patterns that don't serve me to prevent the spiral and anxiety."

—ASHLEY JEFFERSON, founder of The Affirmation T

"Amanda approaches these sometimes-esoteric ideas in a real, honest, and authentic way."

—TAYLOR MOUNT, engineer and artist

ANXIETY TO EMPOWERMENT

About the Author

Amanda Huggins is an author, anxiety and mindfulness coach, speaker, and host of the popular podcast *HealingTALKS with Amanda Huggins*. Amanda's signature scientific, practical, and spiritual approach to anxiety has helped thousands of individuals break out of old patterns and restore peace in mind, body, and soul. She offers her work through one-to-one coaching, digital courses, and retreats. You can connect directly with Amanda on social media @itsamandahuggins or visit her website at www.amandahugginscoaching.com.

CONTENTS

Part One
Anxiety and the
Mind-Body Connection

Part Two
Soul Guidance and Emotional Healing

🦋

Part Three
Embodiment and Empowerment

🦋

EXERCISES

Disclaimer

The information and resources in this book are provided for educational and informational purposes only and are not medical advice. Such information is not intended nor otherwise implied to be a substitute nor replacement for advice, diagnosis, or treatment from a licensed mental health or medical professional. The author and publisher encourage you to consult a professional if you have any questions about the use or efficacy of the techniques or insights in this book.

If you are struggling and need assistance, please reach out for help. There is a resource list provided in the back of this book.

Acknowledgments

I'd like to extend heartfelt gratitude to my family and friends for their unending support throughout the process of writing this book. To my parents, Mary and Brendan, especially: words can't express how invaluable your love and support was, and is. Thank you for the late-night phone calls, constant encouragement, and the unwavering belief in my ability to bring this book to fruition.

I'm wildly grateful for all of the mentors I've encountered throughout my own journey, whose guidance and insights significantly shaped the course of my work. A special acknowledgment goes to Cyndi Dale, whose mentorship and support have been instrumental in my personal and professional journey.

Lastly, to my stabilizing force and constant source of inspiration, Will. Thank you for believing in me, and thank you for loving me exactly as I am.

INTRODUCTION

Navigating anxiety can be an incredibly isolating, confusing, and draining experience. It's not just the physical sensations or the racing thoughts—anxiety also takes an enormous emotional toll on a person. The constant worry, the feeling of being on edge, and the impact anxiety can have on relationships, work, and daily life is overwhelming.

We are living at a time when anxiety is more common than it's ever been before. The fast-paced nature of modern life, the constant bombardment of information, work pressures, social media, and other societal demands all contribute to heightened levels of anxiety. To a degree, anxiety has become normalized: when you scroll through social media, you'll come across memes and jokes about anxiety; if you flip on your favorite streaming service, you'll find tons of TV shows with adorably anxious side characters; have a conversation with a group of colleagues and you're bound to hear someone reference their own anxiety. While it's fantastic that we're seeing increased awareness and more openness about mental health, this normalization of anxiety in today's society also downplays the impact it truly has on people. Anxiety is not just a trend or a minor inconvenience; it's a complex experience that impacts mind, body, and soul.

Anxiety is a lot for one person to manage, and I want to acknowledge and celebrate the resiliency of everyone who faces this silent battle daily. Anxiety may try to convince us that we are weak, but I see it differently. When I witness someone bravely confronting their anxiety and pushing through despite its challenges, I see a person of immense power. Persevering through anxious moments, finding coping mechanisms, and continuing to navigate life are profound testaments to the inner strength we each possess. Anxiety is a heavy burden to bear, and I want to acknowledge the incredible strength and power it takes to continue showing up and moving forward. I also believe there is another kind of power anxious folks can tap into: self-empowerment. Nobody needs to resign themselves to living with high levels of anxiety forever. We all deserve to experience a life that is not overshadowed by anxiety, a life that feels joyful, expansive, and empowered.

Taking control of anxiety is a transformative journey that goes beyond healing; it is a profound practice of self-empowerment. Embracing this path is an act of courage, a bold move toward reclaiming a deep sense of personal power and actively engaging in our own well-being. Each one of us has the capacity to transform our lives by reshaping the way our minds operate—the key is knowing where to begin. When you start digging into the anxious thoughts lurking in your mind, you might unearth a treasure trove of potential. Whether your anxiety is an inner request to heal the past or a little a "soul nudge" asking you to enact change in the present, one thing is for sure: it's trying to get your attention. As you embark on the journey from anxiety to empowerment, you'll discover that your anxious thoughts hold powerful information that actually serves as a guide to creating an amazing life—one that's filled with joy, empowerment, and self-love.

It's important to remember that anxiety is more than a physical sensation, like a racing heart or a pit in the stomach. It encompasses the totality of your being—your physical body, your emotions, and your soul. To truly tune in to the growth that your soul has in store for you, you must start with the body first, then work on your emotional landscape. By first learning how to self-soothe and manage anxious thinking, you can then access the time and emotional space within you to truly heal and embody your empowered self. I know this because I myself have made the journey from anxiety to empowerment.

I struggled with crippling anxiety and a deep sense of misalignment for years, and the lessons I learned on my own path to empowerment ultimately created the perspectives, processes, and exercises that I share with my coaching clients every day. I never planned on becoming a life coach, let alone one who specializes in anxiety. And yet, I work with hundreds of individuals every year through one-on-one work, group programming, and online content. While each person's path to empowerment is unique, I have found there is one truth that applies to everyone I've worked with: true healing happens through an integrative, mind-body-soul approach. My integrative "mind, body, soul" approach to anxiety management wasn't something I intentionally set out to create. Rather, it was a divine byproduct of my own journey from anxiety to empowerment, a result of lived experience that was thoughtfully developed over time.

When I was in my twenties, my life seemed pretty great from the outside looking in: I was driven; I had a fast-paced career in tech; I was well-traveled and always had something fun on my social calendar. But, in reality, I was just an expert-level masker.

I had been caught in the undertow of a silent battle with my mental health for years. At first, my anxiety would visit me in seemingly innocuous moments: after a bad date, while sitting at my desk at work, or after I checked my bank account. Then, my anxiety was always there, omnipresent. What other people saw as "drive" was actually an attempt to stay busy so I could continue running from my emotions. The truth was, I was deeply unhappy about nearly every aspect of my life, and I was so, so afraid that this was all my life had to offer. My confidence was about as sturdy as a house made of Popsicle sticks. In an effort to avoid my anxious thoughts, I'd bounce between destructive and reclusive behaviors, hoping my anxiety would magically disappear.

Eventually, I learned that I wouldn't be able to outrun my anxiety. After yet another visit to rock bottom, I finally committed to taking control of my mental health. I dove headfirst into a bunch of different healing modalities, including therapy, medication, and even self-help books. Traditional talk therapy was a pivotal practice because it granted me the freedom to openly discuss my emotions in a safe and nonjudgmental space for the very first time. I treasured having someone who would hold space for my emotional processing, and I began to build a solid foundation of understanding. Yet, despite this progress, my anxiety remained a constant companion, unwavering in its presence. I then consulted a few psychologists, each of whom recommended prescription medications, including benzos, selective serotonin reuptake inhibitors (SSRIs), and amphetamines. While certain medications did help me feel less anxious, I noticed that I also felt less connected to the rest of my emotions, especially the good ones. I didn't like how "flat" I felt. I decided to go off of medication altogether and instead immersed myself in self-help books that ranged from super-clinical to super woo-woo. I certainly learned a lot about myself in the process, but I couldn't ignore the fact that I'd hit a frustrating impasse: I knew more than ever about the mind and the body, and I had a ton of data points about myself, but I didn't feel measurably different.

I was struggling to find the solution I was yearning for: an actionable, easy-to-digest approach to anxiety management that integrated mind, body, and soul. Individually, therapy, medication, and self-help books worked for a little while, but my anxiety always crept back in, and I felt like I landed back at square one. My healing journey felt like trying to piece together a puzzle without a reference image, and that initial sense of confusion is what inspired me to develop an integrative plan to manage my anxiety. Little did I know that the process I pieced together for my own healing would evolve into my present-day work as a coach.

The multidisciplinary approach I offer to my clients and students combines the science of the human mind with the inherent spirituality of human nature, and it's broken down in such a way that even the most anxious minds can begin to integrate the information and transform themselves. My mission in this lifetime is to share what I've learned about healing with others, and to offer compassionate and soulful support to those who are ready to step into their empowerment. My passion for helping people work through their "stuff" and live from their soul began as one-on-one work with clients, but it has since expanded to speaking engagements, podcasts, and content creation.

In my coaching practice, I have the honor of working closely with individual clients, providing personalized guidance and support to help them navigate their unique journey. In one-on-one coaching sessions, I focus on understanding the needs and aspirations of each of my clients. We work together as a team to identify their healing path, and I support them in feeling, processing, and healing past experiences that have contributed to their anxiety. Empowering my clients to become self-sufficient and confident as they navigate life on their own is also a cornerstone of my work. While I cherish the opportunity to walk alongside my clients, my ultimate goal is to equip them with the skills, insights, and tools they need to stand on their own, fully self-empowered.

In addition to private coaching work, I offer online group programs, self-paced online classes, and workshops that are all designed to support individuals on their path to empowerment. My coaching philosophy centers around the belief that every individual possesses the inherent capacity for growth and empowerment. As a compassionate and dedicated coach, I strive to create an environment where vulnerability is celebrated, self-compassion is nurtured, and self-discovery is embraced. My mission is to empower my clients to tap into their authentic selves, break free from limiting beliefs, and unleash their full potential. Whether it's through intimate one-on-one sessions or transformative group experiences, I am committed to helping my clients live more fulfilling lives. My passion for this work continues to grow as I witness the remarkable transformations that take place when my clients embrace their innate strength and wisdom.

While I love working as a coach, I also have a desire to make my healing work more accessible. The inspiration for this book came from a deep understanding of the challenges that anxious minds face every day. I know that the path to healing can feel overwhelming, and that mental health organizations may seem like daunting labyrinths to navigate. This book as a powerful and actionable entry point into the world of healing anxiety. It's the very essence of my work as a coach, and it includes the lessons, tools, and reflections that have been the most impactful for those I've had the privilege of working with. With the utmost dedication, I have crafted this book to be a guiding light for all anxious-minded souls. This book is broken down into three parts.

Part 1: Anxiety and the Mind-Body Connection

Understanding the biological aspects of anxiety is a crucial step in changing your relationship to it. Part 1 delves into the mind-body connection of anxiety. You'll gain insight into the inner workings of the anxiety "spin cycle," those moments when anxiety seems to spiral out of control. Through self-reflection exercises, you'll learn to recognize the signals your body sends when anxiety is triggered and how to respond in a more empowered way. Somatic exercises will also be introduced, helping you regulate your body's responses and feel more in control when anxiety arises. By gaining a deeper understanding of the biological mechanisms behind anxiety and learning practical tools to manage the mind-body connection, you'll be well-equipped to take charge of your healing journey and transform your relationship to anxiety.

Part 2: Soul Guidance and Emotional Healing

Part 2 explores deeper layers of anxiety by looking beyond the physical sensations. You'll delve into the realms of your soul's inherent wisdom, unlocking a path to healing and empowerment that resonates with you. Mindfulness exercises will help you cultivate present-moment awareness, while cognitive-behavioral techniques will assist you in reframing negative thoughts and beliefs. With the help of additional therapeutic approaches, you'll develop a greater level of emotional awareness, gaining insight into the root causes of your anxiety and learning effective strategies to cope and, ultimately, overcome it. This part of the book will provide you with tools to create positive shifts in your thoughts, emotions, and behaviors, paving the way for a more empowered healing process.

Part 3: Embodiment and Empowerment

In part 3, you'll take the awareness you've gained about your mind, body, and soul and begin the process of integration. This part of the book will focus on developing and maintaining a healthier mindset, one that is aligned with your healing goals. You'll learn how to cultivate a positive attitude that supports your well-being and growth. You'll also explore ways to embody an empowered sense of self while extending compassion to yourself and others. Through practical exercises, self-reflection, and continued use of mindfulness and self-care techniques, you'll foster a new relationship with anxiety and with yourself. This part of the book will empower you to continue the healing process with a renewed sense of confidence and self-awareness.

The work in this book is here to support you on your path toward managing anxiety and cultivating a more empowered way of living. With the help of practical tools, insights, and reflections, you will gain a deeper understanding of your anxiety. It may be a little uncomfortable at times, but growth often requires stepping out of your comfort zone. Embrace the process of self-discovery, and be open to uncovering the hidden gems that lie beneath your anxiety.

This book is small but mighty, and it's not designed to be read cover-to-cover in one sitting. Think of it more like a super-charged, interactive guidebook, one that's filled with lessons as well as exercises for you to explore. Each exercise is designed to be engaging, interactive, and experiential, allowing you to actively participate in your own healing. The exercises provide opportunities for self-reflection, self-awareness, and self-compassion, and they will help you develop a deeper understanding of your emotional landscape. Approach this work at your own pace, taking time to reflect, practice, and integrate the concepts into your daily life.

Throughout this book, you will encounter dozens of journal prompts to engage with. If you don't already have a journal, now's a great time to pick one up. Your journal will become a trusted companion as you delve into this material. It'll serve as a haven for you to capture your thoughts, feelings, and observations as you engage with the information and exercises provided in the book. It will also be a repository for any questions, insights, or realizations that arise along the way.

I understand that journaling may not be everyone's cup of tea, but I encourage you to give it a shot. There's something magical about the physical act of penning your thoughts on paper. It often unlocks truths and insights that might otherwise remain hidden if we were typing or texting our reflections. Let your pen dance across the page, and allow the power of handwriting to reveal your inner world. If finding stillness for extended periods or physically writing feels challenging for you right now, don't worry—there's another wonderful option to explore! Embrace the power of reflection through spoken word by engaging in an insightful conversation with yourself. Use a voice memo to record your musings, allowing your thoughts to flow freely without the constraint of pen and paper. This dynamic approach can be just as effective and liberating, allowing you to express your innermost reflections with ease and authenticity. Whether you choose to speak with your pen or your voice, the important part is honoring your unique journey by finding a method that feels right for you.

Now, it is time to mark the beginning of your journey from anxiety to empowerment! Grab a pen and your journal, and take some time to reflect on how you feel right now. Self-awareness is a powerful tool for transformation, and by capturing your thoughts and emotions at the beginning of this book, you can track your progress and witness your growth over time.

In your journal, answer the following questions in as much detail as you'd like.

- Describe your current experience with anxiety. How does anxiety manifest in your life? How does it impact your mind, body, and soul?
- Why did you pick this book up? What drew you to this material? What is it that you're hoping to learn, understand, or experience? What expectations or hopes do you have for yourself as you embark on this path of self-discovery?
- What emotions are present as you embark on your healing journey? Are you feeling excited? Nervous? Anxious, even? There's no right or wrong answer; use this as an opportunity to acknowledge and validate whatever it is that you're feeling.

Above all, the work in this book is designed to help you deepen your relationship with yourself. And like all great relationships, it requires dedication, communication, and a whole lot of love. I want to close your eyes for a moment. Breathe deeply, and imagine the incredible relationship you can—and will—create with yourself as you embark on this healing journey.

With that picture in mind, write a letter in your journal. This is a letter to yourself, a letter of love, commitment, and dedication to your healing. Pour your heart out. Express your love, admiration, and appreciation for who you are. Share your commitment to your healing and growth, and acknowledge the challenges you have faced with compassion and understanding. Speak to yourself with kindness and encouragement, just as you would to a dear friend or loved one. This is your opportunity to connect with yourself on a deep, heartfelt level, and to affirm your unwavering commitment to your well-being. Be honest, vulnerable, and authentic in your letter. Let the words flow from your heart, and let yourself be seen and heard in a way you may not have experienced before. Embrace this moment as an act of self-care and self-love, and trust that your words will be a powerful reminder of your worth, resilience, and capacity for healing.

When you're done writing, take a moment to read your letter aloud to yourself. Feel the words sink in and resonate within you. This letter is a powerful tool that you can revisit whenever you need a reminder of your own love and commitment to yourself. Keep it in a safe place, and let it serve as a beacon of self-compassion on your healing journey.

I'm immeasurably honored to support you in this process, and I'm so, so proud of you for being here. Let's dive in!

PART ONE

ANXIETY AND THE MIND-BODY CONNECTION

Chapter One
ANXIETY'S NOT JUST
IN YOUR HEAD

In this chapter, we'll explore how to "triage" your anxiety, and we'll find the immediate opportunities for managing those overwhelming feelings. I'll also discuss the importance of the vagus nerve—an indispensable component in the mind-body connection and anxiety regulation. Through meditation, grounding practices, and the magic of the vagus nerve, you'll be one step closer to navigating anxiety with grace.

I'll never forget the moment when I was introduced to the vagus nerve. It was during a yoga teacher training, and as my instructor delved into an anatomy lesson, I found myself utterly confused. For a good two weeks, I couldn't help but think my teacher was saying "Vegas" instead of "vagus." Much to my surprise, the vagus nerve is not, in fact, related to Sin City. It's related to the heart, and to the autonomic nervous system.

The autonomic nervous system (ANS) is responsible for regulating involuntary physiological functions in the body. It controls processes that occur automatically, such as heart rate, digestion, respiratory rate, pupillary response, and more. It essentially manages the body's internal environment, ensuring that it adapts to different situations and maintains a state of balance, or *homeostasis*.[1] The ANS is divided into two main branches: the sympathetic nervous system (SNS) and the parasympathetic nervous system (PNS). Before journeying deeper into the profound healing capabilities of the vagus nerve, let's take a moment to distinguish between these two critical components of our autonomic nervous system.

Understanding the balance between the sympathetic and parasympathetic nervous systems is fundamental to comprehending how our body and mind interact with the world around us. So, let's explore the intricate dance between these two systems that influence our daily lives and sets the stage for the vagus nerve's transformative power.

In our everyday lives, we oscillate between these two nervous systems, the sympathetic and the parasympathetic, without even realizing it. Think of it as a finely tuned balancing act. The sympathetic system revs us up, preparing us for action, while the parasympathetic system works quietly in the background, guiding our bodies back to a state of rest and recovery.

The sympathetic nervous system serves as the body's built-in alarm system. It's the reason your heart races when you're faced with a looming deadline or when you narrowly avoid a traffic collision. But it's the parasympathetic system, our ever-watchful guardian, that helps you return to a state of serenity once the perceived threat has passed. It's like the gentle hand that soothes your racing heart and tells your body, "It's okay, we're safe now."

---

1. *Encyclopaedia Britannica Online*, s.v. "Reflex Actions," accessed October 24, 2023, https://www.britannica.com/science/human-nervous-system /Movement.

The vagus nerve, our main focus in this chapter, is the primary conduit through which the PNS operates its magic. Often referred to as the "wandering nerve," the vagus nerve plays an incredible role in connecting the brain to many of the body's vital organs. It's the channel through which your body communicates with itself, fostering a delicate symphony of balance and harmony.

The vagus nerve is the longest and most complex of the cranial nerves, originating in the brain stem and extending down to various organs in the body, including the heart, lungs, digestive tract, and other internal organs. The vagus nerve plays a crucial role in the body's response to stress and relaxation.[2] It is responsible for helping the body calm down after a stressful event and regulates the rhythm and pace of the heartbeat. In situations like a challenging fitness class, such as yoga or a high-intensity interval training (HIIT) workout, the vagus nerve acts as a behind-the-scenes support system to bring the body out of the fight-or-flight response and restore a sense of calm.

Imagine you're in the middle of a tough workout, and you're feeling physically overwhelmed. Your heart is pounding, you're out of breath, and it feels almost impossible to keep going. Instead of pushing yourself to the limit, you decide to take a quick break to grab some water and take deep breaths. As you take those instinctual deep breaths, something amazing is happening behind the scenes: the vagus nerve is being triggered.

The vagus nerve responds to deep breathing by taking the body out of its fight-or-flight response. It helps stabilize the breath, regulate the heart rate, and restore a state of inner balance. As a result, you start feeling more relaxed, your heart rate returns to normal, and you're able to continue your workout. In essence, the vagus

---

2. Fanselow, "Fear and Anxiety Take a Double Hit."

nerve helps you collect yourself and restores a sense of calm, allowing you to keep going and face a challenge with renewed energy.

The vagus nerve has a remarkable role in helping the body recover from stress and restore balance. It's a powerful reminder of the body's innate ability to self-regulate and find equilibrium, even in the midst of challenging situations. Plus, the vagus nerve doesn't only deal with physical stress—it's critical when it comes to navigating emotional stress too. Your heart rate has to be stable in order to effectively collect yourself and move forward.

Taking time to breathe and process racing thoughts can be a real challenge for those grappling with anxiety. The anxious brain operates at lightning speed, desperately seeking quick fixes to alleviate discomfort. It compels us to search for strategies that "should" quell anxiety, such as distracting ourselves, pushing away anxious thoughts, or forcefully thinking positive thoughts. Yet, more often than not, these attempts prove futile. The reason for this lies in the brain's inclination to prioritize cognitive solutions. Trying to "think positive" in the midst of fight-or-flight mode with an elevated heart rate is like placing the cart before the horse: it neglects the crucial aspect of the body. To effectively address anxiety, it's essential to recognize that the body and mind are interconnected, with the heart playing a significant role in modulating the body's response to stress.

For years, I walked around thinking that my brain was solely responsible for my anxiety. Whenever an anxious thought popped up and my body responded with uncomfortable sensations, I pointed fingers at my brain. My instinct was to tackle the thoughts first, attempting to change them. When this approach didn't work, I found myself growing increasingly frustrated with my apparent lack of control. I convinced myself that my brain was the relentless generator of all negative thoughts and couldn't seem to grasp the positive ones I was trying so hard to create. Little did I know, I was only seeing half the picture. My focus was solely on the cognitive aspect of anxiety, neglecting the profound connection between my brain and my body. This incomplete understanding led me to overlook the crucial roles of the heart and the vagus nerve in regulating anxiety. By honing in on my brain alone, I was missing out on a whole world of opportunities to effectively manage anxiety.

Imagine trying to hold an important conversation with someone while standing front row at an overcrowded, noisy heavy metal concert. That would be a pretty exhausting, ineffective method of communication, and that's exactly what it's like when you're telling the brain to think different thoughts while your body is still in fight-or-flight: there's too much noise happening for any new thoughts to stick. To meaningfully transform your anxiety, start with the heart.

Vagal Nerve Stimulation for Anxiety

The heart is running the show, not the brain. While the brain is responsible for interpreting and processing emotional stimuli, it's the heart that plays a significant role in modulating the body's response to stress and anxiety. Your heart is more than just a muscle that pumps blood; it's comprised of over 40,000 neurons that communicate neurological, chemical, physical, and energetic information to the rest of your body. The heart has even been coined the "little brain," and it sends more electromagnetic signals to the brain than the brain does to the heart.[3] It is a loud, frequent, and powerful communicator. In a sense, the heart is like a

---

3. Alshami, "Pain."

conductor, orchestrating the body's response to anxiety, working in tandem with the brain to help navigate challenging situations.

This means that when the heart rate is elevated, the brain gets inundated by loud, powerful signals from the heart that essentially say, "Hey! We are not safe right now. We are not okay! We need to stop this feeling—*now!*" When the heart blasts some pretty strong messages to the brain, the brain can't take on much new information. This is why "thinking positively" doesn't always work: your brain isn't able to absorb positive thoughts or behavior suggestions because it's busy listening to the heart's messages that say, "We're not safe! We're not safe!" And, in between receiving the heart's messages, the brain is using the rest of its power to figure out how to find (or create) a sense of safety. There's just not space to introduce new information (like positive thinking, mindfulness practices, or behavioral changes) until the heart rate is under control and the body feels a little more grounded.

Before anything else, you've got to learn how to breathe deeply and stimulate that vagus nerve of yours. There are actually quite a few ways to stimulate the vagus nerve, but I like to focus on breathing because, well, most of us don't breathe correctly. When the body is under any sort of physical or emotional stress, most people unconsciously default to shallow, short breaths that are concentrated in the chest area. Shallow breathing isn't necessarily bad; it's a biological instinct that is designed to help when in fight-or-flight. Short, chest-centered breaths bring more oxygen into the body so that if someone was in a dangerous situation and needed to scram, that increased oxygen would allow them to quickly respond to the threat and seek safety. Once they were safe, they would naturally begin to breathe more deeply and their heart rate would slow down. This a great mechanism—when there's an actual threat of danger.

Most of the time, we aren't in actual danger. The anxiety many of us experience on a day-to-day basis is psychosocial, meaning the perceived "threat" that activates the fight-or-flight response is derived from thoughts, memories, and interactions. When anxiety occurs in response to an intangible threat (like thoughts or memories), it's on us to jump in and activate a sense of safety manually. Rather than waiting for "proof" of safety, we must begin that chain of events by taking conscious, slow, and deep breaths to stimulate the vagus nerve.

Let's begin to workshop vagal nerve stimulation. We'll cover a handful of exercises in this section, but we will start with a foundational practice of diaphragmatic breathing. Diaphragmatic breathing, also known as belly breathing or deep breathing, is a technique that involves engaging the diaphragm (the muscle located below the lungs), to take slow and deep breaths. It allows the abdomen to expand when inhaling and contract when exhaling while the chest remains relaxed. This type of breathing activates the relaxation response in the body and takes us out of fight-or-flight. It is a simple yet effective technique that is exactly what it sounds like: you're just going to take a bunch of big, deep breaths through your diaphragm, or abdomen.

Before we begin, start paying attention to how you're breathing right now. Don't do anything to change your breath just yet; I'd like you to notice how you normally breathe when you're engaged in another activity (like reading, for example). How deep into your chest do you breathe when you're inhaling passively? When you exhale, does it feel like you breathe out fully? Make a mental note of how this breath feels in your body. Now, for contrast, let's explore diaphragmatic breathing.

EXERCISE
Diaphragmatic Breathing

1. Sit or lie down in a comfortable position, with your back straight and shoulders relaxed. Place one hand on your abdomen, just below your rib cage, and the other hand on your chest.

2. Start by emptying all of the air in your lungs with a big exhale. Allow the mouth the close.

3. Mindfully and slowly, take an inhale. Focus on expanding the belly first. (Imagine that you're inhaling from your belly button.) The inhalation fills up the belly and diaphragm first, then expands through the rest of the upper body. Imagine that your belly is a balloon. How large can you inflate it? Notice how this feels.

4. Find a slight pause at the top of your breath, enough to let just a *slight* amount of tension build.

5. Exhale and release that tension slowly through the nose.

6. At the bottom of your exhale, ever so gently draw your lower belly toward your spine, as if you could press the last few "drops" of air out of your lungs.

7. Repeat: Continue this slow and deep breathing pattern, inhaling through your nose and exhaling through your nose, for several breaths or as long as you feel comfortable.

Focus on breathing into the lower abdomen, allowing it to expand on inhale and contract on exhale. Pay attention to the movement of the diaphragm, which is located just below the lungs and above the stomach. Pay attention to the quality of your breath as well. Ideally, you will create equally expansive breaths for both inhalation and exhalation. Try not to rush the exhales; those deep, conscious out-breaths are what trigger the chain of command in your body to begin slowing down your heart rate.

———

One of my all-time favorite tools for vagal nerve stimulation is square breathing. What makes it stand out is not only its simplicity but also its practicality. Unlike traditional meditation practices that often require a peaceful and secluded environment, square breathing can be seamlessly integrated into daily activity, whether you're driving, reading emails, or going for a walk.

Anxiety can strike at any moment—it doesn't care about the time or place. Sometimes you find yourself in the middle of an important task or surrounded by responsibilities that don't allow for a twenty-minute meditation. Square breathing becomes your trusted companion during those overwhelming moments, as it can be effortlessly practiced with your eyes open. Its adaptability allows you to engage in the practice even in the midst of hectic meetings, taking care of your kids, or handling work commitments. Imagine skillfully practicing square breathing while discreetly "reading emails" in the corporate world; this breathwork provided me with a sense of calm and control, all while appearing completely composed. Whether you're navigating a traffic jam or amidst the hustle and bustle of a busy day, square breathing grants you access to the profound benefits of vagal nerve stimulation.

EXERCISE
Square Breathing

To practice square breathing, remember the number four. Just as there are four sides to a square, there are four sides to the breath—four is your magic number!

1. Inhale for four seconds.
2. Hold for four seconds.
3. Exhale for four seconds.
4. Hold for four seconds.

If you have a greater lung capacity, you can always extend the length of your breathing to six or ten seconds each. Just make sure to keep all sides of the breath equal, and remember to always practice at a pace and duration that feels comfortable for you.

When practicing square breathing, it's important to aim for equal durations for each part of the breath, including the hold phases. It's common for people to find the holds uncomfortable or tempting to skip, but they play a crucial role in stabilizing the nervous system and maximizing the benefits of square breathing. The holds help slow down your breathing and activate the relaxation response in the nervous system.

If you struggle to maintain focus while square breathing, it can be helpful to visualize the shape of a square forming with each breath: the top line forms on the inhale, the right-hand line on the hold, and so on.

By repeating this practice ten to twenty times (or as long as needed), you will regulate your heart rate, calm your mind and body, and promote a greater sense of relaxation and well-being.

Mindfully Meditating with a Full Mind

Diaphragmatic breathing and square breathing are two wonder-fully simple exercises. These techniques can be practiced virtu-ally anywhere, at any time, and they require no special equip-ment, making them accessible to anyone seeking to enhance their breathing and manage stress levels. These breathing techniques are also a part of my foot-in-the-door approach to get more anx-ious folks meditating!

Many people with anxiety feel resistant to the idea of "clearing the mind" of thoughts in traditional meditation practices. How-ever, meditation is not—I repeat, not—about achieving a clear mind. Sure, you may get there some days, but for the most part, you're still going to have thoughts during meditation. The human brain is designed to think. The true "work" in meditation is to notice when the mind wanders (and starts attaching to thoughts) and practice drawing your attention back to the breath, over and over again. This process of repeatedly redirecting your attention to the breath is a form of mental exercise that strengthens the ability to focus and be present. It's like training a muscle in the mind. With practice, you'll become much better at noticing when the mind has wandered and bringing it back to the breath. The more you draw your attention back to the breath, the more you're going to breathe. And the more you breathe, the greater your chances are of getting out of fight-or-flight.

If you've never meditated, or if you're a self-proclaimed "bad" meditator, I ask that you hear me out: meditation in its simplest form is just breathing. You already know how to do it. In fact, you're kind of an expert at it already! I think mainstream society has made meditation seem way too complicated. It's often built up as a serious, difficult, or solemn practice designed to achieve a perfectly clear mind. But meditation doesn't have to be complicated. It doesn't have to be about achieving some elusive state of mind, and it's definitely not about forcing yourself to clear your mind of all thoughts. Meditation really can be as simple as paying attention to your breath, becoming present in the moment, and simply observing what happens without judgment.

So, let's start with a beginner-friendly, powerful meditation: The "I Am" Mantra Meditation. Mantras are simple sounds, words, or affirmative statements used to focus the conscious and subconscious mind in meditation. All the while, you'll be breathing deeply and encouraging the body to enter the parasympathetic nervous system. If you breathe for long enough, the brain should relax enough to begin receiving and accepting the mantra you're repeating. I like to use "I am" mantras because they're as powerful as they are simple. When you're already swimming in anxious thoughts, powerful and simple practices—ones that don't require much additional brain power—are your best friends.

EXERCISE
The "I Am" Mantra Meditation

Before beginning the meditation practice, take a moment to check in with yourself. Place a hand on your heart, close your eyes, and ask yourself, *How am I feeling right now?* Take a moment to acknowledge and identify the emotions and sensations associated with your anxiety. Is there an adjective that sums up how your anxiety feels in this moment? For example, you might tune in to yourself and notice that you're feeling ungrounded, unsafe, or fearful.

Once you've identified that adjective, take a moment to reflect on what word might replace it. Think about how you would like to feel instead. You might come up with a clear, equal, and opposite adjective, such as *safe* if *unsafe* was the initial feeling that came up. However, don't feel limited to choosing a word that conveys the exact opposite. If you chose an adjective like *fearful*, you don't necessarily have to choose something like *courageous*; maybe instead of fearful, you'd like to feel trusting, peaceful, or protected. Let your intuition guide you toward a word that feels right.

Next, plug the word you've landed on into the following sentence: "I am _____." This is now your mantra for this meditation, and you're ready to dive in. Please read through the following steps in full before starting your meditation.

1. Set a timer for this practice. If you're new to meditation, aim for five minutes. If you already have a well-developed meditation practice, set your timer for ten to twelve minutes.

2. Position yourself comfortably, whether lying down or sitting up. Allow the eyes to close, and soften any tension in the lower belly.

3. Take a few minutes to simply rest in that relaxation before bringing attention to your breath.

4. On your inhales, repeat to yourself (out loud or in your mind) "I am."

5. On your exhales, say the word that you chose.

6. As you slowly draw in and release your breaths, practice cultivating the feeling or experience of your statement. A mantra like "I am powerful" may feel different than "I am joyful," even if that difference is subtle. Whatever word you

choose, make a genuine attempt to create the feeling, and give yourself permission to surrender into it fully in mind and body.

7. When the timer goes off, give yourself a moment or two to pause in gentle reflection as you return to your body. If any significant feelings or insights came up, jot them down in your journal before jumping back into your day.

Grounding and Getting Back into the Body

Anxiety can have a profound impact on the body and our perception of it. When anxiety kicks in, you may become hyperaware of the physical sensations happening in your body. Your heart might be racing, your palms sweaty, your breathing shallow. You may feel a sense of heightened tension, as if your body is on high alert. On the other hand, anxiety may also trigger an overall feeling of numbness, leaving you feeling disconnected from your body and the outside world. It's as if your body is there, but your awareness is elsewhere. You may feel detached or dissociated from your own physical sensations, as if you're watching your body from a distance.

In either situation, you're no longer "in" your body—you've become ungrounded. When you're ungrounded, your mental attention is scattered and you'll feel a level of disconnect between your mind, your body, and your surroundings. This mind-body disconnect can make it difficult to focus, execute tasks, or make decisions, even after the initial anxiety trigger is long gone. The solution? Get back into your body by utilizing grounding practices.

Grounding techniques work by taking the attention off your physical anxiety and shifting your awareness back to the present moment. These practices are a great complement to the breath-work and meditation suggestions outlined earlier in the chapter; all of these practices work together to support the nervous sys-tem's relaxation response. Here are three of my favorite ground-ing exercises that can be done almost anywhere, at any time.

EXERCISE
Progressive Body Relaxation

Progressive muscle relaxation involves tensing and then relaxing different muscle groups in the body, one at a time. This technique can help to release physical tension, promote relaxation, and bring you back to the "now."

1. Begin by taking a few deep breaths, focusing on the sen-sation of your breath moving in and out of your body. If it feels comfortable, you can close the eyes.

2. Starting with your toes, tense the muscles in your feet by curling your toes downward. Hold this tension for a few seconds, then release and relax the muscles completely.

3. Move up to your calf muscles and tense them by pulling your toes toward your shins. Hold this tension for a few seconds, then release and relax the muscles completely.

4. Repeat this process of tensing and releasing each muscle group in your body. Move up from your thighs to your stomach, chest, back, arms, hands, and finally your face

and scalp.[4] As you tense each muscle group, focus on the sensation of tension and the feeling of the muscles contracting. Then, as you release and relax the muscles, focus on the sensation of relaxation and the feeling of the muscles becoming loose and limp.

5. When you've finished, allow yourself to relax completely, feeling the tension and stress leave your body.

6. Spend a few moments simply resting and focusing on your breathing, feeling the sensation of your breath moving in and out of your body.

7. When you are ready, slowly open your eyes and take a few deep breaths before getting up and resuming your daily activities.

Go slow with this practice. Allow yourself ample time to focus on each part of the body. For added grounding support, I like to place one hand on my heart, which promotes reconnection to the Self and offers a sense of comfort to the body. Incorporating some form of self-touch (whether it's a hand placed on your heart, your arms wrapped around you in a hug, or something else), can promote a deeper sense of security and relaxation in the body. For example, in the early days of my own battle with anxiety (and specifically, when my anxious attachment was acting up), I vividly remember how vulnerable my heart space felt. As I attempted to ground myself back into my body, I experi-

---

4. There may be places in the body where you can't activate muscle tension (for example, the earlobes). Don't skip those spots! When awareness is placed on those areas of the body, imagine the sensation of tension and relaxation there. Some of my other favorite places to practice this imaginary tension and relaxation: the skin on the back of your neck, the tip of your nose, and the webbing in between your fingers and toes.

enced a sense of discomfort, almost like my heart was physically exposed. During those moments, I found solace by gently placing a hand on my heart, which helped me relax.

EXERCISE
The Five Senses

The Five Senses is a classic grounding tool that is both effective and easy to remember. This exercise brings attention to the present moment and one's physical surroundings by methodically engaging all five senses. By focusing on specific objects, sensations, sounds, smells, and tastes, the mind and body begin to reconnect, which creates a sense of grounding.

1. Take a few deep breaths and focus on the sensation of the breath moving in and out of the body. With each breath, anchor yourself in the present moment, feeling fully connected to your body.

2. Look around the room and identify five objects that you can see. Focus on each object and try to describe it in detail in your mind. For example, if you see a book on a shelf, you might think about the color of the cover, the texture of the pages, and the title of the book.

3. Next, identify four things that you can feel. This might include the sensation of your feet on the ground, the texture of your clothing against your skin, or the feeling of air moving across your face.

4. Identify three things that you can hear. This might include the sound of a fan or air conditioner, the hum of traffic outside, or the sound of birds singing.

5. Identify two things that you can smell. This might include the scent of flowers, the smell of food cooking, or the smell of your own perfume or cologne.

6. Finally, identify one thing that you can taste. This might include the taste of a drink or food that you are consuming, or simply the taste of your own saliva in your mouth.

7. Take a few deep breaths and allow yourself to become fully present in the moment, noticing the sights, sounds, smells, and sensations around you.

I still use this exercise today, especially when I'm out in public and feeling overstimulated. Sometimes the sheer size of a new environment (like a concert venue or a big city) becomes overwhelming. Using this technique breaks the environment down into smaller, less overwhelming pieces.

EXERCISE
The Five Photos

The Five Photos is my modernized take on The Five Senses technique. While the classic Five Senses technique relies on the environment to anchor us in the body, The Five Photos technique introduces a modern twist by harnessing the power of digital photography and positive memories to create an even more profound sense of grounding.

In this fast-paced digital age, smartphones have become gateways to cherished memories and moments of joy. By curating a selection of digital photos that capture your happiest and most uplifting experiences, you can carry a portable gallery of positivity with you everywhere you go. This gallery serves as a powerful tool for reconnecting to your true self. The Five Photos technique utilizes the sense of sight by incorporating images that evoke a symphony of emotions. Each photograph becomes a portal to a time when joy, love, and contentment enveloped your being, reminding you of your inner strength and resilience.

This technique invites you to create a personal photo gallery that serves as a portal to the body. Here's how to do it.

1. Create an album on your phone that contains five photos or videos that make you feel safe, loved, or happy.[5] These could be photos of loved ones, pets, places you enjoy, or anything else that brings you joy. When narrowing down your photos, focus on the images that elicit the most immediate, positive emotional responses. Choose photos that make you say, "God, that was such a good day," or that instantly remind you of a happy memory.

2. The next time you're feeling ungrounded, open up this album. Look at one image, taking a few moments to focus on the details and the emotions that it brings up for you. If the photo evokes joy, see how much of that joy you can bring back into your body just by staring at the image. Allow yourself to be fully immersed in the photo and the feelings it evokes.

3. Repeat this process with all five photos, allowing yourself to fully engage with each one and the emotions they bring up for you. Continue to breathe deeply as you immerse yourself in the positive feelings that the photos trigger.

---

5. If you can't find five photos that bring up feelings of love and safety, treat this album as a vision board instead! Find a few images on Google or Pinterest that are soothing, relaxing, or inspiring to you, and use those.

4. When you have looked at all five photos, put your phone away and take a few more deep breaths to focus on the feelings in your body.

This tool can be a powerful way to quickly ground yourself in moments of anxiety or disconnect. By carrying a digital album of five specific photos that you know will bring you feelings of safety, love, or happiness, you can access these positive emotions when you need them most.

These Practices Are the Starting Point

Ideally, when you practice any grounding or meditative technique, you'll do so in a comfortable and quiet place where you have the safety to really relax. If that's not possible (say you're at work, or hanging out with a friend), you can still practice these techniques, though some creativity or adaptation might be necessary. Back when I was working in the corporate world, I would take a "trip to the bathroom," where I'd spend about five minutes practicing muscle relaxation behind the stall door. Rather than practicing full-body muscle relaxation, I'd spend those five minutes only focusing on the places where I was storing the most tension: my upper back, neck, and jaw. An abbreviated version of *any* of the techniques in this chapter can still be powerful. If you can only find five minutes to breathe or ground, *use* those five minutes! Your body and mind will thank you for it.

Chapter Reflections

The following questions are designed to help you explore the roots of your anxiety and the methods you've used in the past to soothe or heal it. Reflect on what has been effective and what hasn't, and contemplate the reasons behind those outcomes.

Additionally, consider the practices in this chapter that resonated with you and sparked excitement, as they will play a crucial role in supporting your anxiety management going forward. Your answers to these prompts will help you develop a deeper understanding of your unique journey and the healing that awaits you.

- When did your own anxiety begin?
- What have you done in the past to try to soothe or heal your anxiety?
- What worked, and what didn't work? Why?
- What practices from this chapter are you excited to use to support your anxiety management?

Chapter Summary

Meditation and grounding exercises are a form of anxiety "triage"; they're tools that can used as an immediate opportunity to manage your anxiety. The work starts in the body, by addressing the heart, so that there's enough space for you to actually create meaningful change within the mind. This is the most effective way of combatting (and, ultimately, healing) the dreaded "anxiety spin cycle," which we'll address in the next chapter.

Chapter Two
THE SPIN CYCLE

Understanding the relationship between the heart, brain, and breath is an important first step on the journey to anxiety management. We start with the body so we can then begin to work with the mind. I've found this is the most effective way of combatting, and ultimately transforming, the dreaded "anxiety spin cycle."

The "spin cycle" is how I refer to the seemingly endless (and particularly dramatic) kind of anxiety loop, where one benign thought escalates into a full-blown freak-out. At peak freak-out, one might start to catastrophize, shut down, or react in a way they're not proud of, all of which further fuel the anxiety. Spin cycles feel like an endless loop, and the challenge for many folks is that sometime it's hard to recognize they're in one until it's too late.

I'm sure you've had your fair share of anxiety spin cycles, just as I have. They used to come out of nowhere and swallow me whole. One moment, I'd be sitting at my desk writing a to-do list for next week, and out of nowhere—*bam*. My brain decided that not only would I never get through my to-do list, I'd probably never

RE-TRIGGER
Continued reactivity can "confirm" fear-based
stories. It hinders your ability to mindfully
observe and respond to anxious thoughts,
making it eaiser to reengage in the spin cycle.

OBSERVATION
The observation of a person, place, thing,
or thought. When someone observes
something, the brain decides if its
safe (good) or unsafe (bad).

REACTION
Now that your body and
brain are locked into the
"reality" of a negative
emotion or beliefe, you
react from that space. You
might not like your
reactive patterns, but they feel
automatic or uncontrollable.

SENSATION
When the mind determines
the observed experience is
"bad," the body's
parasympathetic nervous
system is activated. The heart
rate increases, and the physical
anxiety sensations set in.

EMOTION
Now that all of those anxious
thoughts have been stirred up, a negative or
fear-based emotional responce is activated. This
is where the anxiety really starts to take root in
the body: Anxious thoughts are no longer just
thoughts. They've created meaning, and that
meaning begins to (falsely) inform your identity.
Ususally, these emotions are rooted in stories.

THOUGHT
Now that the sympathetic
nervous system is activated, the mind and
body are set on seeking safety. The mind
will examine negative outcomes and create
thoughts that seek to solve or alleviate the
threat. If no good option is identified, the
mind will keep searching.

The Anxiety Spin Cycle

finish anything in my life, because I was the World's Biggest Failure
and nobody loved me.

Of course, none of those thoughts were true. Going from
creating a to-do list to "nobody loves me" is a pretty big jump,
but that's what happens when an anxiety spin cycle takes over!
Anxious thoughts will jump quickly and chaotically, they'll create stories, and they'll convince the body to believe those stories.
But the good news is, it's possible to learn to spot the cycles when
they begin, diffuse their impact, and maybe even dissolve some
of the spins altogether.

In this chapter, I'll start by breaking the spin cycle down step-by-step to help you understand what's really going in the mind and body when you start to spin. In chapter 3, we'll explore a few handy-dandy tools and journaling prompts to help break out of the spin cycle. To begin, take a look at the following diagram, which outlines the six phases of the spin cycle: Observation, Sensation, Thought, Emotion, Reaction, and Re-Trigger.

Observation

Observation happens when we see something, think something, or remember something. This begins as a fairly neutral experience: observing anything is neither good nor bad; it's simply what you're doing. But as the mind observes a thought, the brain takes that information and begins labeling those observations as either "good" (safe) or "bad" (unsafe). As you learned in the previous chapter, if the brain decides that the observation is unsafe, it alerts the heart, which then communicates to the rest of the body that it's time to go into fight-or-flight mode.

The way the brain observes and interprets experiences is profoundly shaped by our unique life journey and the emotional patterns we've developed over time. Let me share an example from my own life to illustrate this point. During my formative years, my first romantic relationship was marked by control and verbal abuse. In order to keep the "peace," I would often acquiesce to my then-boyfriend's bids for control over me. I found myself limiting time with friends and seeking approval for my activities and interactions. Whenever I dared to deviate from his demands by spending time with friends or making choices for myself, I was met with shame, anger, and emotional withdrawal as "punishment" for not conforming. This triggered my fight-or-flight response, plunging me into hours or even days of attempting to regain his approval. When I was able to get back on his "good" side, my nervous system registered that the threat of upsetting him was gone, and some of my anxiety would temporarily dissipate. To further cope with the anxiety-provoking situations, I developed strategies. I tiptoed carefully to avoid upsetting him and steered clear of any situation that risked his disapproval. Over time, my nervous system concluded that experiencing his displeasure was unsafe, leading me to adopt coping mechanisms like people-pleasing and self-minimization to create a semblance of safety within myself. As long as I didn't upset him, I was safe. My body began to associate my own freedom of choice (like choosing to be myself, hang out with my friends, and engage in my own interests) with a lack of safety. So, whenever I observed that I was doing something that would upset my boyfriend, I'd re-engage in the anxiety spin cycle.

Sensation

From a biological perspective, this reaction is actually an adaptive response to perceived danger. When the brain perceives a threat, it triggers a cascade of physiological responses aimed at preparing us to fight or flight. The adrenal glands release hormones such as adrenaline and cortisol, which increase blood pressure, heart rate, and breathing rate. Blood is shunted away from non-essential organs such as the digestive system and redirected toward the muscles, which are primed for action. Basically, if there is a real threat, the brain wants to plan for what's next, and your body is preparing to run.

If someone were to experience a genuine threat to their life (say, being chased by a tiger), their body would naturally activate the fight-or-flight response to help them survive. Once the threat is no longer present (for example, they saw the tiger being swallowed by a crocodile), the brain would acknowledge that information and communicate it to the body. From there, the body would take anywhere from twenty to sixty minutes to naturally come out of the fight-or-flight response.

But most people aren't in fight-or-flight because they're getting chased around by tigers—they're anxious because of thoughts and memories stored in their mind. When it comes to anxiety triggered by thoughts or memories that are not in the present moment, the body may have a harder time recognizing when it's safe to come out of fight-or-flight because it doesn't see the threat leave.

Unlike a real physical threat, anxious thoughts or memories can linger in the mind, keeping the body in a heightened state of alertness even though there is no immediate danger. If the thought is still there, the threat is still there. This prolonged activation of the fight-or-flight response can contribute to ongoing feelings of anxiety, stress, and unease. The body remains on high alert, with stress hormones circulating, muscles tense, and the mind racing. The body's natural ability to return to a state of calm may be impaired, as the perceived threat (in the form of the lingering thought or memory) continues to trigger the fight-or-flight response.

Thought

If the tiger discussed in the Sensation section was really chasing after someone, the Thought phase would be a lifesaver. In a life-or-death situation, the anxious mind will swiftly analyze potential escape routes and solutions to evade harm. However, in modern times, the majority of anxiety we experience isn't triggered by genuine threats of physical harm. Instead, it arises from psychosocial sources, where the perceived dangers are often rooted in emotional responses and stories. While the mind's instinct to search for solutions remains intact, the objects of our fears are now more intangible and complex.

Unlike the immediate danger posed by a wild animal, psychosocial anxiety emerges from a different realm. It can be triggered by social interactions, emotional vulnerabilities, unresolved traumas, or the fear of failure, rejection, or judgment. As a result, the mind's search for a resolution can become a never-ending loop, leading us down a rabbit hole of anxious thoughts and worries. It's as if our mind is tirelessly searching for answers to an abstract puzzle, one that cannot be easily solved with conventional strategies.

Let's look at my first relationship again. My fear-driven pattern of making myself small so as to not upset my boyfriend solidified the thought that when I could keep the peace and make people around me happy, I was "good"—even if it was at the cost of my own freedom of choice. If I were to ever upset someone else (especially if I upset someone just for being who I was) I was "bad," and my nervous system would feel extremely unsafe. Over time, a piece of that story became a part of my core identity: I craved approval, and without it, my body and brain would both feel deeply anxious and unsettled.

Eventually, that core narrative manifested as an anxious attachment style. I remember when I had first moved to Los Angeles in my early twenties and began casually dating a charming daytime-TV actor. It wasn't serious for either of us, but we both enjoyed the occasional dinner or brunch together, and it was nice to have someone to talk to. One day, we were texting back-and-forth to make plans for the following weekend when all of a sudden, he stopped responding. A few minutes went by, and then a few hours—and it sent me into a tailspin. My heart rate skyrocketed, I felt shaky, and I was obsessively rereading our texts and checking his social media, searching for clues as to where I went wrong. I felt crazy. My intellect "knew" that in the grand scheme of things, a few hours without a response wasn't actually a big deal, but my body and brain were still freaking out.

The subconscious anxiety programming from my first relationship came rushing back, causing my mind to fixate on the idea that I must have done something wrong to not receive a response. Based on my past experience, my nervous system misconstrued the lack of a response as a threat, thus triggering my anxiety attack. My brain interpreted the silence as a "punishment," and my obsessive social media scanning was my mind's way of trying to find answers and create emotional safety again. If I could just find a reason why this person hadn't responded, or proof that I hadn't done something wrong, maybe then my nervous system could relax. So I scrolled, and scrolled, and scrolled, because the anxious mind will search for solutions until the body feels better again. The tricky part about anxiety, of course, is that the relentless searching usually leaves the body feeling even more distressed and overwhelmed. The sought-after "solution"— whether it's a text back, or a clue on social media—remains elusive. It's like being caught in a loop of uncertainty that exacerbates anxiety instead of providing relief.

Emotion

In my case, anxious thoughts like *What did I do wrong?* transformed into an emotional response: "I believe I've done something wrong by being myself, and now I feel scared, bad, and unworthy." These emotions were so pervasive, and I felt powerless over them. Each incoming anxious thought reinforced my negative beliefs about myself. As I wallowed in these emotions, the thoughts of my own inadequacy grew, which only reaffirmed the negative perception I had of myself. I was no longer "experiencing" emotions, I was identifying *as* the emotions, thus setting me up for the next phase of the cycle.

Reaction

The intensity of my emotions had me believing that I was, indeed, unworthy, and I began to react to the world around me as if that were true. Because I held a deep-seated story about my unworthiness, I would overcompensate by seeking external validation and people-pleasing. My reactions were often driven by a fear of rejection or abandonment, leading me to sacrifice my own needs and desires in order to maintain a sense of safety and acceptance. In those moments of reactivity, I would become hyperaware of how others perceived me. I desperately wanted to be liked, admired, and seen as competent, so I would go above and beyond to prove my worth to others. However, this constant striving for external validation only reinforced the belief that I was inherently inadequate. Because I wasn't present to this cycle within me, the pattern persisted.

When there's a lack of presence to the thoughts and emotions that the anxious brain has created, it's almost guaranteed that one will react from the negative emotion rather than respond from a place of clarity. Responding might look like mindfully deescalating the thoughts, self-soothing, or choosing a different approach. When you are reacting, on the other hand, you'll engage your anxious, familiar patterns in a way that feels both out of alignment and out of control. Emotional reactivity can show up intrapersonally (nobody around you sees or knows that you're in an anxious response, but you know) or interpersonally (your reactivity affects other people).

Re-Trigger

When someone reacts from a place of anxiety rather than taking a pause to regulate their nervous system and emotions, they're more likely to reinforce the negative beliefs they hold about themselves. This will exacerbate the anxiety they're already experiencing, and it creates an endless cycle of retriggering.

In my case, the more I reacted to my anxiety, the more I believed that I was inherently flawed and unworthy. Each time I responded with fear and avoidance, it served as "evidence" that my anxious thoughts were valid and accurate. The fear-based stories gained strength and became deeply ingrained in my belief system. This vicious cycle kept me trapped in a self-fulfilling prophecy. My reactivity fed into my core narratives of not being good enough or deserving of love and success. As I continued to react from a place of anxiety, I inadvertently reinforced the very patterns that fueled my anxious thoughts and emotions.

Pop Quiz: Where Can You Break the Cycle?

So, there it is—the anxiety spin cycle in all its complexity. It may seem overwhelming, and you might be thinking, *This entire cycle happens in just a matter of seconds. How on earth am I supposed to break free from this relentless cycle?!* I get it. The anxiety spin cycle can indeed come on swiftly and fiercely, but I l assure you that breaking free from its grip is possible. In fact, there are two crucial phases within this cycle where you can begin to regain control, and in a moment, we'll explore those specific phases in more depth.

Before we do that, though, I want to empower you to use your critical thinking skills first. Based on what you've learned so far, take a guess: which two phases do you think will offer you the best chance of breaking the spin cycle? I'd also like you to also reflect on why you think your selections are right. Write your responses to the prompts below in your journal.

- I believe the first best place to break the anxiety spin cycle is the _____ phase because…
- And the second best place to break the anxiety spin cycle is the _____ phase because…

Now, let's find out if your guesses (and your reasonings) were right.

The two best phases to break the spin cycle are the Sensation phase and the Thought phase. If those were your two guesses, congratulations! You're spot-on, and we'll discuss the reasoning shortly. If one of your guesses was the Observation phase, you're not necessarily wrong. In a perfect world, you would be able to nip a spin cycle in the bud right when you observe something triggering: you'd notice the trigger, let it go, and return to normal without getting anxious. But, alas, it's not always that simple. If you're already worked up and anxious, it's really, really hard to just let go when you've observed an anxiety trigger.

Breaking a spin cycle at the Observation phase is certainly something to work toward, but it's a challenging place to start. Breaking the spin cycle at the Sensation and Thought phases is more accessible for long-term change. Let's break down the why and how of it all.

Sensation Phase: Breaking the Cycle When You *Feel* Something

My use of the word *sensation* refers to all the icky, uncomfortable ways anxiety manifests in the body: a racing heart, a pit in the stomach, a feeling of dizziness or tightness. You're already in the spin cycle by the time you start feeling the physical sensations of anxiety, but you can interrupt the spin by recognizing and soothing those physical sensations. When you're able to interrupt the physical sensations of anxiety—which takes practice—you'll lessen the overall intensity of your spin and bring the body back to a resting state more quickly.

Often, people will experience different physical sensations based on what's triggering their anxiety. For example: romantic anxiety may be felt in your stomach or heart, whereas anxiety about the future may be felt at the top of your chest and neck. Each and every body is unique, and how your anxiety physically manifests may be completely different than someone else's. Your job is to understand the patterns of anxious sensations in *your* body. Here is a checklist of common physical sensations that are associated with anxiety. Go through the list and check off which physical symptoms most frequently accompany your anxiety.

- Racing or pounding heart
- Sweating or chills
- Shortness of breath or difficulty breathing
- Nausea or upset stomach
- Headaches or migraines
- Muscle tension or tightness
- Trembling or shaking
- Dizziness or lightheadedness
- Chest pain or discomfort
- Fatigue or exhaustion
- Difficulty sleeping or insomnia
- Restlessness or feeling on edge

- Numbness or tingling sensations in the body
- Hyperventilation or feeling like you can't catch your breath
- Panic attacks or feelings of intense fear or terror
- Digestive issues such as irritable bowel syndrome (IBS) or acid reflux
- Skin conditions such as eczema or psoriasis
- Changes in appetite, either overeating or loss of appetite
- Irritability or mood swings
- Inability to concentrate or focus
- Other: _____

EXERCISE
Sensation-Shifting Breathing

In times of heightened anxiety or overwhelming tension, it's crucial to have a gentle yet effective tool to release those uneasy sensations and create a sense of calm within. That's where Sensation-Shifting Breathing comes in. This powerful exercise invites you to connect with your body's wisdom and use the breath as a conduit for transformation.

Through a series of simple yet impactful steps, you'll tap into the healing power of visualization and breathwork to release tension and anxiety. As you engage in this practice, you'll witness the mind's ability to transform uncomfortable sensations into feelings of ease and lightness. So, find a quiet space and let the soothing rhythm of your breath guide you as you embark on this journey of sensation-shifting for inner peace.

1. Close your eyes and begin to breathe deeply. Place one hand on your heart and the other hand atop your body, somewhere you feel tension.

2. Begin to visualize a white light moving in through your nostrils as you inhale. Imagine that white light filling up your entire heart space (and wherever else you're feeling anxious sensations).

3. Hold your breath for a moment, and in your mind's eye, imagine that light scrubbing away the tension you're feeling. (I always like to imagine those little guys from the Scrubbing Bubbles commercials, excitedly sweeping, scrubbing, and cleaning to their heart's content).

4. As you exhale, watch that light move out of your heart space and away from your body. As it leaves, see it taking away the tension you've been feeling. Watch and, most importantly, *feel* the sensations begin to dissipate.

5. Repeat this breathing pattern for at least five to ten minutes.

By bringing attention to the sensations you're feeling, you're essentially creating a "speed bump" for the spin cycle. Sensation-Shifting Breathing (SSB) trains you to notice the feelings in your body so that you can mindfully begin to deescalate the anxious thoughts building up inside you. Breath and visualization are a powerful, powerful combination! In some cases (especially when you're experiencing low-grade anxiety), SSB may create enough space for you to fully release anxious thoughts and sensations and move on with your day. When you're battling more intense anxiety, however, SSB alone won't be enough. In order to break through more intense spin cycles, you've got to begin tackling your thoughts. You'll learn more about that later on in this chapter.

Other Tools to Soothe the Spin Cycle

While breathwork is a fantastic option for soothing anxiety, it isn't the only one. There are numerous other methods that can help reduce sensations of anxiety and support the body's exit from fight-or-flight. Different methods work for different people, so it's important to find what works for you personally. Incorporating additional techniques into your routine can create a more comprehensive approach to anxiety management. Think of breathwork as your baseline, then play with introducing other tools that meet your needs.

WEIGHTED BLANKETS

One of my favorite tools for self-soothing is a weighted blanket. These blankets are filled with materials like beads or pellets, which provide gentle pressure and create a sense of comfort and safety. Weighted blankets work by providing deep touch pressure, which is a form of tactile sensory input that reduces anxiety and promotes relaxation. This pressure stimulates the production of serotonin, a neurotransmitter that is associated with feelings of well-being and happiness, and also reduces levels of cortisol, the stress hormone.[6]

Research studies have shown that the use of weighted blankets can lead to improved sleep quality, reduced anxiety and stress levels, and improved mood. For example, a study published in the *American Journal of Occupational Therapy* found that using a weighted blanket led to significant reductions in anxiety and physiological arousal levels in adults with anxiety disorders.[7] Another study found that using a weighted blanket led to

---

6. Noyed, "Weighted Blanket Benefits."
7. Eron et al., "Weighted Blanket Use."

improvements in sleep quality and reductions in the amount of time it took participants to fall asleep.[8]

If you don't have a weighted blanket, or if it's not in your budget right now, create a makeshift weighted blanket using things you already have lying around your home. Use extra blankets, beanbags, or other soft materials that are able to add some weight or pressure.

EFT TAPPING

Emotional Freedom Technique (EFT) tapping is a self-help tool that can help reduce anxiety symptoms. EFT tapping involves methodically tapping on specific acupressure points on the body while focusing on a specific issue or problem. This technique helps rebalance the body's energy system and reduces the emotional impact of negative experiences. EFT tapping has effects similar to that of weighted blankets: one study found that tapping can help reduce anxiety symptoms by increasing activity in the parasympathetic nervous system.[9] EFT tapping also directly stimulates the vagus nerve, which you now know plays a key role in regulating the body's stress response. The best part? EFT tapping is completely free—all you need is your body—and it can be done at any point in time. I've practiced EFT tapping at work, during social gatherings, and even while on the subway!

To practice EFT tapping, start by identifying a specific issue or problem that is causing anxiety. If you're unable to identify a specific trigger or reason why you're anxious, that's perfectly fine as

---

8. Baric et al., "The Effectiveness of Weighted Blankets on Sleep and Everyday Activities."

9. König et al., "How Therapeutic Tapping Can Alter Neural Correlates of Emotional Prosody Processing in Anxiety."

well; in that case, bring your awareness to the experience of anxiety itself. Then, begin tapping methodically on specific acupressure points while breathing deeply. The acupressure points are as follows: the gamut point (the fleshy part of your hand between your wrist and your pinky finger, the part of your hands you'd use to make a "karate chop" motion), the top of your head, the inner corners of your eyebrows, the sides of your eyes, underneath your eyes, under your nose, your chin, and your underarms.

Here is a diagram that serves as a visual point of reference for these acupressure spots. You can also do a quick search on YouTube for guided EFT tapping tutorials.

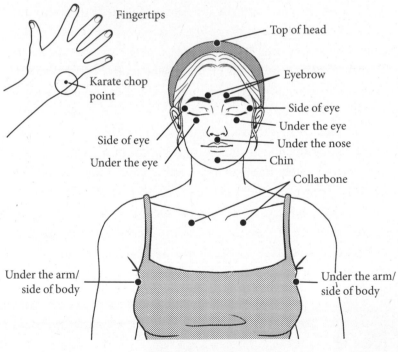

EFT Tapping Chart

Another place I recommend practicing EFT tapping on is your thymus gland, which is located in the center of your chest behind the breastbone or sternum. This is one of my favorite spots to tap because of how inconspicuous it is: you can tap with just one hand without drawing any attention to yourself. In the past, when I'd get anxious at social gatherings, I'd start tapping my thymus, sometimes even mid-conversation with someone!

You can choose to repeat a mantra as you tap and breathe, such as "I am safe," or you can simply focus your attention on your breathing.

Yoga and Gentle Movement

Movement can also be a powerful way to soothe the body. Gentle forms of exercise like yoga or light stretching can release physical anxiety and promote relaxation. Yoga, in particular, is a powerful tool: the combination of deep breathing and gentle movements can activate the body's relaxation response, leading to a decrease in heart rate. In addition, yoga has been shown to increase levels of gamma-aminobutyric acid (GABA), a neurotransmitter that helps regulate mood and anxiety.[10] There are a number of styles of yoga you can choose from, but I find yin yoga classes to be the most supportive for anxiety reduction.

Yin yoga can be especially helpful for those dealing with anxiety, as the slow, meditative nature of the practice can help quiet racing thoughts and soothe the nervous system. Yin is a slow-paced style of yoga where poses are held for longer periods of time (typically three to five minutes or more), often with the support of props like blocks and bolsters. The goal is to release

---

10. Streeter et al., "Effects of Yoga versus Walking on Mood, Anxiety, and Brain GABA Levels."

tension in the muscles and connective tissues of the body, and to cultivate a sense of stillness in the mind.

Many yin poses focus on deep hip stretches. It's thought that stressful or traumatic experiences can cause the hip muscles to go into subtle flexion, and if the hips aren't regularly stretched, that tension (and the emotions associated with it) doesn't get to be released. It's not uncommon for tears or waves of emotion to bubble up during deep hip stretches; it's a mind-body-soul release of the tension that's accumulated over time. I had that experience myself, long before I understood the nuances of how we carry energy throughout the body. During one of my first yoga classes over a decade ago, the teacher cued us into pigeon pose, which is a deep hip stretch, and kept us there for about a minute. The pose was uncomfortable, and I used my breath to soften my body into the discomfort. After one big exhale, I experienced a swell of emotions bubble up, and they began to pour out of me through tears. At first I was confused, because I wasn't necessarily sad in that moment, but what I was experiencing was a release of old grief, sadness, and pain that had been stored in my hips.

If you don't have a yoga studio in your area (or you're feeling too anxious to be in public settings), you can practice yin yoga poses at home. Do a quick search of "Yin Yoga for Anxiety" on YouTube or Instagram, and you'll find hundreds of tutorials that you can follow along with from the comfort of your living room. You also don't need to do a long practice to reap the benefits of yin yoga poses; the next time you're triggered and your body needs some self-soothing, try one or two of the following poses.

These poses should be held for several minutes each, which will allow your body to fully relax into the stretch. If it feels safe, close your eyes and place your awareness in the center of your heart while you focus on your breathing.

Supta Baddha Konasana (Butterfly Pose)

This pose provides a gentle stretch of the hips and is also thought to support better sleep.

Start by lying on your back with both feet planted on the ground about hips-width distance apart. Walk both feet together to touch, then let the knees splay out on either side of you. For added support, you can place pillows, blankets, or bolsters underneath the knees. Bring one hand to your heart and the other to your low belly. Breathe deeply, and imagine the anxious energy melting out and away from your hips. Stay in this pose for three to five minutes.

Balasana (Child's Pose)

This pose activates your parasympathetic nervous system and allows your body to relax back into a state of rest. It also offers a gentle hip stretch.

Kneel on the floor and rest your seat atop your heels. Open the knees wide, and drop your torso in between the legs. Extend your hands out long on the mat in front of you, with your palms on the floor facing down. Allow the center of your head to rest on the mat. Breathe deeply, and focus on feelings of safety. Stay in this pose for three to five minutes.

Viparita Karani (Legs Up the Wall Pose)

When you're anxious, blood vessels constrict and cause blood to flow more slowly throughout the body.[11] This pose helps restore healthy circulation and blood flow.

Sit on the floor and scooch your bum until it's flush against the wall. Lie back and extend both feet up the wall above you so

---

11. Abraham, "How Anxiety Can Create Circulation Problems."

that your legs are vertical. You can stay here, or you can add a hip stretch by moving the legs into a V shape, keeping the backs of your legs flush against the wall. Focus on feelings of relaxation, and visualize any energy that's been lost returning to you. Stay in this post for five to twenty minutes, paying attention to how your body responds.

Some people experience "pins and needles" or a tingling sensation in the legs due to this shift in blood flow. If this occurs, or if you begin to feel dizzy or uncomfortable, exit the pose.

Savasana (Corpse Pose)

This is the ultimate relaxation pose—your body gets to release all effort and simply be.

Lie on your back. Have both feet at least hip-distance apart. Let both arms rest on either side of you with the palms facing up. If you're feeling especially triggered, place one hand on your heart and focus on the feeling of connecting to yourself. Stay in this pose for as long as you'd like.

YOUR ENERGY CENTERS

Your chakras, or energy centers, are each associated with different emotional and physical states. By becoming aware of the physical sensations in your body, you may be able to glean additional information about your anxiety based on where those feelings are located and which chakra that area corresponds to. For example: Let's say that when your anxiety gets triggered, you feel the most physical sensations in your gut or belly area. The chakra that corresponds to this region of the body is the solar plexus, which is associated with confidence, self-worth, and feelings of empowerment. You can deduce, then, that part of your long-term healing will have to do with balancing the emotions and energies of this chakra.

Noticing where physical sensations are located in your body can be a helpful way to understand which chakras may be pointing you toward healing. If you're unfamiliar with the chakra system, here is a brief guide that illustrates where the seven main chakras are located, as well as their emotional and physical associations.

Crown Chakra

Responsible For: Spiritual connection; connection to the Higher Self and the Divine

Anxious Physical Symptoms: Headaches; disorientation; sensitivity to light and sound

Anxious Emotional Associations: Feeling alone in the world or universe; feeling emotionally or energetically overstimulated and shutting down

Third Eye Chakra

Responsible For: Intuition; perception; insight

Anxious Physical Sensations: Headaches; sinus issues

Anxious Emotional Associations: Inability to trust self; difficulty concentrating; difficulty envisioning the future

Throat Chakra

Responsible For: Clear, loving communication and expression; inner listening (with self) and outer listening (with others)

Anxious Physical Sensations: Sore throat or laryngitis; frequent loss of voice

Anxious Emotional Associations: Challenges with self-expression; over-sharing or fear of sharing; speaking inauthentically

Chakra Figure

Heart Chakra

Responsible For: The ability to receive and express love; compassion and love for self and others; ability to forgive and to release judgment; ability to offer grace

Anxious Physical Sensations: Heart palpitations; tightness of chest; difficulty breathing

Anxious Emotional Associations: Being closed off, judgmental, or harsh to self or others; high amounts of self-created pressure or expectation; feelings of constantly failing self or others

Solar Plexus Chakra

Responsible For: Personal power; confidence; self-esteem

Anxious Physical Sensations: Digestion issues; persistent sinking or "pit" in stomach

Anxious Emotional Associations: Feelings of unworthiness; self-judgment

Sacral Chakra

Responsible For: Creativity; sexuality; ability to move through emotions

Anxious Physical Sensations: Sexual dysfunction; lower back pain; urinary problems; reproductive system issues

Anxious Emotional Associations: Guilt; shame; lack of self-worth

Root Chakra

Responsible For: Grounding; stability; survival instincts

Anxious Physical Sensations: Restlessness; lower back pain; leg or feet problems; adrenal issues

Anxious Emotional Associations: Fear; insecurity; sense of not belonging; ungroundedness

———

Take a few deep breaths and scan your body from head to toe, paying attention to any areas of tightness, discomfort, or tension. Take note of where you feel these sensations and see if you can connect them to one of the seven chakras listed. With practice, you may find that you become more in tune with your body and better able to identify and address any imbalances in your energy centers.

If the concept of chakras or energy centers doesn't resonate with you, don't worry—you'll still address the emotional healing needed to resolve physical sensations as you progress through this book. On the other hand, if this section piqued your interest and you'd like to learn more about chakra healing, there are thousands of fantastic books and resources available. My own teacher, Cyndi Dale, has dozens of books available on the chakra system that are a great starting point. You can find a list of recommended resources in the back of this book.

Thought Phase: Breaking the Cycle
When You *Think* Something

One indicator that you are in an anxiety spin cycle is a racing mind. The mind runs rampant with stories when you're in a spin cycle, but they likely aren't rooted in reality. If you're able to recognize these anxious stories, you will be able to deescalate the spin cycle faster. This takes practice.

Let's imagine a scenario together.

Imagine that you're the groundskeeper of an beautiful, abundant garden, and you've got a big weed problem. Not only do weeds grow extremely fast, they can grow almost anywhere, and the garden has been overtaken by weeds. As groundskeeper, you already know that just trimming the weeds or pulling a few leaves here and there isn't enough to manage the problem. If you want the weeds gone, you've got to rip 'em out at the root.

So, that's exactly what you do! You get to work, patiently weeding your garden until the grounds are pristine once again. As much as you'd like to get the job done in one day, you know that's just not possible: the garden is enormous, and the weeds are everywhere. You break up your work over the course of the next few weeks. On days where you have a little more energy, you might spend an extra hour or two weeding. Other days, you might be busy or a little drained, but you still pull a few out. And maybe you lose a few days to rain, but it's no big deal. Day by day, you mindfully chip away at your task. It's arduous labor, but it's the kind of work that elicits a big swell of pride once it's finished. And eventually, you do finish!

For months, there's not a stray leaf in sight. You're sure you've finished the job completely—until a few months later, when you notice new weeds have appeared. As the groundskeeper, what will you do? Will you throw in the towel and quit your job? Decide that your garden is an absolute failure? Give up on nature altogether, and swear to never set foot outside again? Probably not. In all likelihood, you'll say, "Looks like a few new weeds are cropping up. I'll go pluck 'em." It isn't that big of a deal; not only is it your job, it's just how gardens grow.

If the human mind is a big, beautiful, bountiful garden, your anxious thoughts are the weeds. Just like a garden, our minds can sometimes be overrun with anxious thoughts, the metaphorical "weeds" we've got to extract. The goal isn't to create a perfectly weed-free mind forever, but to gradually clear out the stories that our anxious brain has created. This might feel overwhelming at first, but with the help of the "Truth versus Story" framework, it becomes easier to distinguish between reality and the stories we tell ourselves, leading to greater clarity and anxiety management. Before we get into it, let's look at what I mean by "Truth versus Story."

- A truth is an unaltered experience. It has no energetic charge, no emotion, and nothing attached to it. It's simply an understanding of what happened, without any assumptions or exaggerations. It's raw fact.

- A story is all of the other stuff that the anxiety brain has decided is happening, with little-to-no evidence based in reality. Stories are charged with emotion and are formulated based on our past experiences or fears. In this way, they can feel like truth—but they're not.

I understand how challenging it can be to separate truth from story when you're deep in a spin cycle. But here's the key: once you understand the distinction between truth and story, you gain a powerful tool to untangle yourself from the grip of anxiety. By learning to identify and challenge the stories your anxious brain creates, you can start to separate fact from fiction and make more informed and rational choices. This is where the "Truth versus Story" framework comes in handy, helping you navigate through the web of anxious thoughts and emotions with clarity and discernment.

Years before I became a coach, I worked in content marketing at a handful of different technology startups. While I enjoyed the excitement and energy of these environments, there was always an ever-present threat of job insecurity looming over me. In my experience, when a startup faced financial constraints, content marketing was often the first department to face cuts. This reality fueled my anxiety and triggered a barrage of stories in my mind about losing my job, an uncertain future, and financial instability. It was challenging to separate the truth from the stories my anxious brain was creating, and I found myself caught in a spiral of worry and fear.

One of the companies I worked for had gone through a pretty rough couple of months, so of course, I decided that I was going to do everything in my power to not get fired: I'd show up extra early, work extra hard, do whatever I could to prove I was invaluable. One morning, I was at my desk nice and early, typing away—and definitely hoping to impress my boss. To my absolute horror, when my boss walked through the office doors, he walked right past me without as much as a hello. He just dropped his briefcase down, let out an exasperated sigh, and started working. Naturally, my anxiety concluded that this twenty-second interaction (or lack thereof) meant that I was getting fired later. I began rationalizing that story: My boss didn't say hello to me because he must feel guilty about having to fire me later. All of that sighing was probably because he's stressed out, knowing he'll have to take on all of my work once I'm gone. Worse yet, maybe we're *both* getting fired!

I sat at my desk, consumed with panic and worry, as my mind spiraled. The looming uncertainty of my financial situation and the shame of potentially losing my job had taken over my thoughts. I spent the workday in panic, though I got very little work done. My heart felt like it was going to jump out of my chest, and I was so anxious that I didn't even attempt to examine my thoughts or regulate my breathing. In fact, because I was so sure I was going to be let go, I spent most of the day trying to preparing a new resume and rehearsing the speech I'd have to give to my parents. Then, something happened: I received a calendar invitation from my boss to "chat" at 5:00 p.m. Anyone who has worked in a corporate job knows that a 5:00 p.m. "chat" is rarely a good thing.

However, when I finally sat down with my boss, I was taken aback to learn that I was not, in fact, getting fired. Instead, he had called me to his office to actually chat! During that conversation, I learned that he had a pretty difficult morning: he'd gotten into a fender bender right before pulling into the parking garage, and he was still frazzled when he walked into the office. Because I had not had that context, and because my mind was already predisposed to thinking the worst, I had spent the entire day creating a story that had no grounds in reality. In that moment, I realized how many stories and assumptions my anxious mind had created without solid evidence. The truth was simple: my boss didn't say hi to me, and he appeared to be stressed. That's it. That stress had nothing to do with me. But do you see how quick I was to create a story? And how quickly I let that story take over my entire day?

This is probably a familiar narrative to many anxious folks. How many times have you found yourself in a similar situation, where you've become totally wound up by an assumption? Practicing "Truth versus Story" begins the metaphorical "weeding" process. Each and every time you can come back to truth, you're training your mind to stop automatically diving headfirst into stories. You're learning how to deescalate catastrophic thoughts and detaching from worst-case scenario. You're disrupting the spin cycle.

EXERCISE
The Truth versus Story Framework

The next time you're triggered, actively practice separating truth and story. The following questions will help you distance yourself from the drama of the anxious mind and come back to clarity. Pro tip: write these questions down in the "Notes" app of your phone, too. That way, you can easily address your anxiety on the fly, with or without your journal.

1. What just triggered my anxiety?
2. What stories is my mind creating right now?
3. What is the truth? What's really going on in this moment?
4. What is my best next step to serve my mind?
5. What is my best next step to serve my body?

Those last two questions are important, because they're grounded in mindful action.

Asking yourself a question like *Is there a next step I can take? Is there a way to gather more information about my perceived stressor?* might eliminate some anxious spirals altogether. For example, if I were versed in practicing "Truth versus Story" during the firing fiasco and I had asked myself the question *What is my next best step?*, I probably would have just talked to my boss and nipped the whole thing in the bud. If I could go back in time, I would have pulled him aside. We had a great rapport, and I probably could have gotten away with being super honest and just asking him, "Hey, am I getting fired?" Or, in a more professional way, "Hi! I saw you put a meeting on my calendar toward the end of the day. Is there anything I can do to prepare, or can you share additional context on the meeting subject matter?" This might seem like a no-brainer to someone who doesn't struggle with anxiety, but logical thinking doesn't come naturally when you're in the spin cycle—which is exactly why you've got to proactively practice this work until it does become second nature.

Once you've located truth, you must commit to staying there. When your anxiety brain wants to drag you back into a spin cycle of negative thoughts, breathe and come back to the facts. For example:

- Your friend doesn't hate you because they didn't return your call. They just didn't return your call yet.

- You're not a bad parent because you forgot to pack your kid's lunch. You just forgot to pack their lunch.

- You're not going to be alone forever because that one person rejected you. It just didn't work out with *one* person. (One person! Out of billions of other humans on the planet!)

When you don't have all of the facts, distract! Now, I'm not suggesting avoidance or running away from an issue that needs to be addressed, but the human mind wants to work. If you don't give your mind a job, it's going to find one (and that "job" is likely going to be revisiting anxious stories and playing them on repeat).

Imagine you just found out you might have two equally important obligations on the same day: your best friend in the world just told you she's most likely going to set her wedding date for April 21, which is the same day as your sister's graduation from law school. They're both meaningful, important events that you always planned on attending, but now you're freaking out about which one you'll choose. Your automatic response might be to start spinning in anxiety, fretting over the many ways you're going to inevitably let someone down. Instead of allowing yourself to go down that rabbit hole, you could practice Truth versus Story. Here's what that might look like.

- **What just triggered my anxiety?** I just found out I have two conflicting events. Not only do they both mean a lot to me, I'm really afraid of hurting someone based on the choice I make.

- **What stories is my mind creating right now?** No matter what, someone is going to be really mad at me. No matter what, I'm going to make the "wrong" choice.

- **What is the truth? What's really going on in this moment?** Well, I actually don't know for sure that these events will conflict. My best friend said she "might" choose April 21 for her wedding date. And, I suppose, even if both events are on the same day, the timing of the events might not conflict. I don't have all of the information yet.

- **What is my best next step to serve my mind?** Because I don't have all of the information yet, the most I can do is share that I may have a conflict and request to be looped in when more information is available. It doesn't serve me to keep running through every possible scenario until I have more facts. When I do, I will commit to exploring all options from neutrality rather than negativity.

- **What is my best next step to serve my body?** That whole conversation just gave me a headache, and my entire body feels tight. I think I'll take a nice bath when I get home and meditate for a few minutes to clear out some of this pre-emptive stress my body is holding on to.

I want to emphasize that coming back to truth is distinctly different from toxic positivity. This isn't about pretending an anxious thought doesn't exist, or trying to "be positive" and mask the truth of what you're feeling. Finding truth is about grounding yourself in the reality of *what is actually happening* so that you can keep yourself from dropping into the spin cycle. Creating that space for yourself sets the stage for the deeper, more soulful work ahead: understanding why these anxious patterns exist within you at all, and learning how to work with those patterns for self-transformation.

Chapter Reflections

Now that you've delved into the intricacies of the anxiety spin cycle, it's time to reflect on the application of this information in your own life. Read through the following questions, then close your eyes and breathe deeply as you explore what comes up. To find the answers, pay more attention to your body and your breath than your brain.

- When you're anxious, where do you feel the most sensation in your body?
- What does it feel like? (For example: heat, tightness, dizziness, etc.)
- About how long do those physical sensations last?
- Do different triggers manifest differently in your body?
- Is there any other information you can glean about the sensations in your body when you're anxious?

Write your responses in your journal to help crystallize your observations. The more you know about your body, the better equipped you'll be to recognize when you're in a cycle so you can do something about it. The next time you're feeling your special brand of anxious sensations, your number-one job is to create as much safety and comfort for your body as possible. By now, you know that deep breathing is a fantastic way to create safety in the body, so you can build on that practice by using the power of visualization, "seeing" your breath flowing in and out of the parts of your body that are uncomfortable. For example, let's just say you've just received a text from your partner that really didn't sit well with you. You can feel your heartbeat racing, your breath has gotten shallow, and you can sense a growing tightness in your chest. Because your full-blown anxiety spin probably hasn't set in yet, this is a great place to practice what I call Sensation-Shifting Breathing (SSB). This breathwork practice is a way to reintroduce mindful awareness when you first begin to notice anxious sensations in your body.

Chapter Summary

The anxiety spin cycle is best interrupted during the Sensation and Thought phases. Sensations of anxiety or activation in the body are a cue to practice self-soothing techniques. When the anxious mind begins creating stories, this is a cue to seek out truth. Practicing the "Truth versus Story" framework consistently will train the mind to examine the negative thought patterns that are created by anxiety.

Chapter Three
SLEEP STRATEGIES TO TAME ANXIETY

One of the most frustrating and exhausting ways anxiety can manifest in the body is through sleep disturbances. Perhaps you've found yourself in the same cycle I did: I'd come home from work, exhausted beyond belief and eagerly looking forward to a good night's rest. But, the moment my head hit the pillow, I found myself wide awake as my mind raced with thoughts, worries, and anxieties. The more I needed sleep, the more elusive it became. With each hour that passed, I'd recalculate how much time I'd have left to rest if I could just fall asleep at that moment. I'd lie awake in bed for hours, and I'd be even more drained and depleted the next day.

A bad night of sleep can trigger the beginning of a vicious cycle. In addition to waking up feeling groggy and unfocused, the brain is actually more predisposed to anxiety the next day. Lack of sleep has significant impact on the brain's ability to regulate anxiety.[12] Without enough deep rest, the medial prefrontal cortex (the part of the brain that's responsible for emotional regulation)

---

12. Goldstein and Walker, "The Role of Sleep in Emotional Brain Function."

doesn't get a chance to restore. This means that after a night of little to no sleep, the brain is at a disadvantage, so it becomes more challenging to manage any existing anxiety. Hear me when I say this: healthy sleep care is self-care. Healthy sleep care is emotional care. Someone can have all of the tools in the world to manage their anxiety, but without proper, consistent rest, it will feel like an uphill battle.

I understand that sleep can be an emotional topic for some people. It's really, *really* frustrating to read about the importance of getting good sleep if you struggle to achieve it. It's understandable to feel frustrated, especially if better sleep is something you've been working toward for a while but still aren't seeing any results. You are not alone in this struggle: sleep eluded me for years, and I've worked with dozens of clients over the past decade who once shared this challenge. Both myself and the clients I've worked with have since developed healthier sleep patterns, and I'm proud to report that I now get a healthy eight hours of sleep a night on a regular basis—a far cry from where I was years ago. My intention in this chapter is to help you create the framework to get a good night's rest too. Whether you're currently striving to improve your sleep or you're among the fortunate ones already enjoying restful nights, there's something valuable in this chapter for you. With time, patience, and a bit of grace, creating healthy sleep *is* possible.

Creating Healthy Sleep

"Healthy" sleep isn't just about the amount of hours someone snoozes for—it's also about the quality of sleep. Researchers have found that dreamless sleep, or non-rapid eye movement sleep (N-REM), is a natural anxiety inhibitor.[13] When the brain accesses N-REM, heart rate and blood pressure drop, and the body is able to truly rest and restore. A broken sleep schedule or nights filled with vivid dreams (REM sleep) don't have the same positive impact on the brain and body that deep sleep does. Intense, vivid dreams indicate that the subconscious mind is active, and because the mind also engages in emotion during a dream state, the heart rate won't lower quite as much. This isn't to say that having a ton of vivid dreams is a bad thing; it's just a signal that there's a lot on the subconscious mind, and as a result, there's less access to restorative sleep.

Creating healthy, restorative sleep naturally can be boiled down to two things: creating better routines and addressing the overall emotional dysregulation that disturbs rest. The latter will be addressed as you make your way through this book. In this chapter, we'll focus primarily on creating better sleep habits.

Morning Routines

Preparing for sleep begins the moment you wake up. That might sound a little extreme, but preparing for sleep isn't just about the actions taken in the evening before bed; it's also about the choices made throughout the day. Great sleep starts with a morning ritual that grounds you and connects you to your mind, body, and soul. Grounding yourself in the morning sets you up to *stay* connected to yourself throughout the day and better manage any stress or anxiety that comes up. You're setting yourself up for improved anxiety management, which in turn prepares you for a better night of rest.

---

13. Simon et al., "Overanxious and Underslept."

We live in the age of the influencer, and it seems like *everyone* has a morning routine to share. Some of the ones I've seen are pretty elaborate. Don't get me wrong, I'm all for a slow, grounding morning filled with matcha, journaling, yoga, meditation, and a homemade smoothie, but it's unrealistic to expect that *that* kind of morning can happen every day with consistency. For folks who spend their mornings getting ready for work or taking care of children, elaborate morning routines are aspirational at best. It's easy to get swept up in the idea that a morning routine needs to be complex, but the truth is, the best morning routine is one that can be done consistently, is tailored to your lifestyle, and meets your unique needs.

Because morning routines are so important, it's usually one of the first things I'll ask a new client about. If they don't have a solid routine in place (especially if they've struggled to find the time within their busy lifestyle), we'll talk through their challenges and find solutions together. My client Cindy is a great example of this. Cindy is a mom of three boisterous boys and co-owns a thriving business with her husband. Her average morning used to be a blur of answering emails, responding to urgent texts, and getting two of the three kids to school on time. Cindy was lucky if she could find a few spare minutes to brush her hair, let alone squeeze in a lengthy morning routine. She figured if she couldn't find the time to accomplish an "ideal" morning routine, it wasn't worth trying at all.

Together, Cindy and I focused on finding and using the time she *did* have, even if it was just five minutes. A grounding morning ritual isn't about how much time it takes, it's about how that time is used. The true value of a morning ritual lies in its ability to center you and prepare you for the day ahead.

There are three key components to a great morning ritual.

1. **It's time that is proactively set aside, just for you.** This is especially important for those who are constantly on the go and focused on the needs of others. It's beneficial to create small slices of time to check in and reconnect with yourself.

2. **It's something that grounds you into your body.** This can be as simple as light stretching done with intention, or closing your eyes and breathing deeply. The point is to focus on being present and connecting with your body.

3. **It's something that allows you to set the tone for the day.** While grounding into your body, you can choose to set an intention that serves as a framework or guidance system. If you become ungrounded at any point throughout the day, you can call yourself back to this intention.

Just one activity can accomplish all three components. Your morning routine can be drinking your first cup of coffee, going for a walk around the block, or even just sitting on the closed toilet seat in your bathroom—which was what Cindy chose to do at first! In her case, being a mom of three meant that alone time was hard to come by, so she'd find her five minutes of grounding during her first trip to the bathroom each morning. It was the only place her youngsters wouldn't bother her. The longer she maintained those five conscious minutes of time, the more she realized how beneficial it was for her. Soon, those five minutes became ten, and ten became fifteen. Her boundaries around time and self-prioritization shifted as she noticed how much better she felt throughout the day.

Reflections on Morning Routines

Take a moment to pause and reflect on your morning routine, for it holds the potential to shape the trajectory of your entire day. Journaling on the following prompts will offer you an opportunity to gain clarity and insight, guiding you toward a more intentional and empowered start to the day.

- Do you have any false or unrealistic expectations about what a good morning routine "should" look like? If so, can you let go of those expectations?
- How much time can you commit to each morning with consistency?
- What will your grounding practice be?

In the fast-paced reality of everyday life, unexpected challenges can quickly derail us. A grounding morning routine can help to set a deliberate and mindful pace for the day ahead, which allows you to better manage your overall stress and energy levels throughout the day.

Grounding opens up a dialogue between your brain, your mind, and your body, but this dialogue should continue throughout the day. To maintain that open line of communication, reflect on the following prompts.

- What are the signs throughout the day that tell you that you're feeling exhausted? How do these signs manifest in your body and mind?
- What are your current daily habits and routines that contribute to your exhaustion? Are there any habits that you could adjust or eliminate to help manage your exhaustion better?

- What activities or practices help you feel energized and revitalized? How can you incorporate more of these activities into your daily routine?

- How do you currently respond to moments of exhaustion or fatigue during the day? Do you push through them or take a break? Are there more effective ways to manage these moments of fatigue?

- How do you prioritize rest and relaxation in your life? What are some adjustments you can make to ensure that you're making time for rest and rejuvenation?

Remember, this is an ongoing and evolving dialogue with yourself. As you continue to explore these questions, you'll gain a deeper understanding of your needs and discover new ways to support yourself throughout the day.

Exploring the Mental Aspect of Sleep

When it comes to developing healthy sleep habits, it can be easy to get caught up in the "how" before a healthier routine can be established. You might start with commitments like "I'll try to go to bed an hour earlier each night" or "No checking my phone past 9:00 p.m." only to last a few days before returning to your old habits. Without your "why," those well-intended commitments to yourself are unlikely to be maintained.

Connecting to a deeper emotional motivation can be a powerful tool for sticking to your sleep goals. Take a moment to reflect on why sleep is important to you. Besides your intention to better manage your anxiety, why *else* does getting better sleep matter to you? Take some time to reflect on your personal reasons for wanting better sleep.

- Is it because you want to feel more energized during the day, be more in flow at work, or be more present with your loved ones?
- Is it because a well-rested you is able to show up to their life better? If so, in what ways?
- What does a well-rested you look like?
- What other important parts of your life will improve when you commit to creating better sleep?

Whatever your answers are, keep them in mind as you work toward developing a healthier sleep routine. Connecting to your "why" will help you stay motivated and committed to prioritizing your sleep health.

Developing Personal Accountability

The hardest part about creating better sleep hygiene is learning how to slowly reduce, and ultimately quit, your existing bad habits. And there's one big, bad habit that nearly all of us are guilty of, it's aimless scrolling on social media. Late-night scrolling is a triple threat: it impacts your time, your emotions, and your brain. Every website or app has its own algorithm, and it is the algorithm's *job* to keep you scrolling for as long as humanly possible. The longer you scroll, the more likely it is to come across content that can trigger anxiety and negative emotions. Once you're activated—even if subtly—the mind will start to ruminate, and you'll to experience those pesky intrusive thoughts that make it harder and harder to fall asleep. Additionally, the blue light emitted from all that device scrolling disrupts your body's natural production of melatonin, the hormone that regulates sleep.[14] By exposing

---

14. Chang et al., "Evening Use of Light-Emitting eReaders."

yourself to this light, you're essentially telling your brain that it is still daytime, which can interfere with your body's natural sleep-wake cycle.

I know how tempting it can be to reach for your phone and do one last scroll through Instagram, TikTok, or YouTube before lights out, but if you want to sleep well, you have to commit to reducing or eliminating social media exposure before bed. I understand that this is a tough habit to break. Coming back to the "why" you previously identified will come in handy and help you commit to establishing a new nighttime relationship with social media.

Developing a healthier routine is an incredible step toward better sleep, but it's important to remember that consistency is key. Just like any other habit, it will take time and repetition for our bodies to adapt and for our minds to form new patterns. Our bodies have a natural circadian rhythm that functions optimally when we maintain a consistent sleep schedule, so if you've been struggling with inconsistent sleep patterns for a while, it's important to be patient with yourself as you work toward establishing a new routine. Your body may need time to readjust to the changes you've made. It's crucial not to give up if you don't see immediate results. Developing healthy sleep habits is a journey that requires persistence and dedication. Remember to be gentle with yourself during this process. It's okay to have setbacks or slip-ups along the way. The key is to keep going and stay consistent with your sleep rituals. Celebrate small victories and progress, and don't be too hard on yourself if you have a night of poor sleep. It's all part of the process.

A good pre-bed routine serves as a transitional phase: it marks the end of the day's activity and signals to the brain and body that it's almost time to relax. Your pre-bed routine can be simple or elaborate, but it should be tailored to your needs and preferences. Use the following reflection prompts to examine your relationship with rest and start building better sleep routines.

Reflections on Sleep Routines and Sleep Hygiene

- **When it comes to sleep, where do you break your own boundaries, and why?** Is "one last video" *really* one last video? Do you often find yourself pushing your bedtime back? Do you push your bedtime so far back that you have to sacrifice or readjust parts of your morning routine the next day? For example: "I'll just stay up until 1:00 a.m.— which means I probably won't have time to go to the gym tomorrow."

- **How do those broken boundaries affect your routines and mood the following day?** Do you take ownership of the mishap and course-correct your behaviors the next evening, or do you displace ownership and hope that something will change the next day?

- **Examine your sleep "should" statements.** These are statements you think to yourself but don't always follow through on, such as "I should really limit my caffeine intake, or I should stop drinking water right before bed so I'm not waking up every few hours to pee." For each of your "should" statements, write out a tangible action step that you can hold yourself accountable to. For example, buy a measured water bottle that you drink throughout the day to reduce the pre-bed water-chugging that disrupts your sleep cycle. The tangible action steps you come up with should be simple and easy for you to follow through on.

- **Create your new intended boundaries for sleep.** Keep the following things in mind as you craft your new boundaries.
  - What is your intended social media cutoff time, and what is your intended sleep time? These two times should be separate. (I suggest cutting off social media at least ninety minutes before your intended bedtime.)
  - Are there any dietary changes you'd like to make? For example: switching from coffee to tea, limiting alcohol consumption, or drinking more water throughout the day.
  - What is a replacement activity you can integrate in place of your social media scrolling? If you don't have something else planned, your brain will simply go back to the pattern of scrolling. Come up with a few accessible, simple transitional activities that won't activate your nervous system, such as journaling, reading a book, or tidying up your space.
  - What is your new overall sleep schedule? What time will you go to bed, and what time will you wake up? If possible, aim to create a schedule that allows for about eight hours of sleep each night.

Naps Count Too!

Adult naps are underrated, and they shouldn't be! If you're struggling with sleep at night, there's no shame in squeezing in some extras z's on the weekends, or even on your breaks from work. Napping can provide you with an opportunity to catch up on restorative sleep, even if it's just for a short duration. And, contrary to popular belief, napping can actually boost productivity and performance. Like sleep, napping has been shown to improve cognitive function, including memory, learning, problem-solving, creativity, and decision-making.[15] A short nap can recharge your brain and enhance your ability to focus, concentrate, and retain information. It can also help improve performance in tasks that require quick thinking—like responding to stress or anxiety. So, even if you're struggling to sleep at night, a well-timed nap during the day can help boost your cognitive function and keep you sharp and alert.

When you're sleep-deprived, your body produces more stress hormones such as cortisol, which can negatively impact your mood, immune function, and overall health.[16] Taking a nap can help lower cortisol levels, relax your muscles, and promote a sense of calm, reducing stress and anxiety, even if it's just a brief nap during a hectic day. Napping can also have a positive impact on your mood and emotional well-being. It can help you to turn a bad day around and, like deep sleep, can also help you manage negative emotions more effectively.

Tips for a Successful Nap

Keep the following tips in mind the next time you want to catch up on some rest. These simple yet effective strategies will help optimize your sleep experience and ensure you wake up feeling refreshed and rejuvenated.

- **Keep it short.** Aim for a nap duration of twenty to thirty minutes to avoid entering into deep sleep, which can leave you feeling groggy.
- **Find a conducive environment.** Choose a comfortable, quiet, and dark environment to help you relax and fall

---

15. Lovato and Lack, "The Effects of Napping on Cognitive Functioning."
16. Leproult et al., "Sleep Loss Results in an Elevation of Cortisol Levels."

asleep faster. If possible, avoid napping or getting too cozy on your bed. Remember, effective naps are supposed to be short!

- **Be consistent.** Try to nap at the same time each day to help regulate your body's internal clock and establish a routine. Everyone's sleep needs are different, so experiment with different nap durations and timings to find what works best for you.
- **Avoid napping too late in the day.** Napping too close to bedtime can interfere with your nighttime sleep. Aim for a nap in the early afternoon. (Maybe you can squeeze in a twenty minute nap instead of that 2:00 p.m. coffee!)

If you don't consider yourself a napper, don't throw these tips away. Even if you don't fall asleep, lying down in a quiet environment for twenty to thirty minutes *still* has benefits. This is called "Non-Sleep Deep Rest," or NSDR, a term coined by Stanford neuroscientist and researcher Dr. Andrew Huberman. NSDR is a type of rest achieved when the body is in a state of deep relaxation but the mind is still awake, also known as the *theta brain wave state*.[17]

Many anxious folks get caught up in the idea of sleep itself. Taking the focus away from "sleep" and shifting it to "rest" takes the pressure off of *needing* to fall asleep. Without that preoccupation, it becomes easier for the mind and body to actually drop into a state of relaxation. When you're in such a deeply relaxed state, your brain waves will shift from the beta frequency, a state of high brain activity, to the theta frequency, a deep, meditative

---

17. Visit www.nsdr.co to learn more.

state of relaxation.[18] When you're in a theta brain wave frequency, your body has a chance to self-restore. A state of NSDR can be achieved by following the napping tips shared earlier.

If you find you're still antsy and can't get the body to relax, try incorporating a practice such as Progressive Muscle Relaxation, which was shared in chapter 1 of this book. Progressive Muscle Relaxation will bring your focus back to your body and help you consciously release tension from head to toe. Then, simply give yourself a chance to rest in that stillness.

To further support your relaxation, turn on some binaural beats. Binaural beats are a type of auditory illusion created by listening to two slightly different frequencies in each ear, which results in the brain perceiving a third, "phantom" frequency. Binaural beats are believed to affect brain wave activity, including the production of theta brain waves. When listening to binaural beats, your brain naturally synchronizes its own brain wave activity with the frequency of the binaural beats, resulting in a shift toward a more relaxed state. The effectiveness of binaural beats may vary from person to person. If you find they don't seem to work for you, or if the music is too distracting, you might work better with brown noise or pink noise. You've probably heard of white noise before; it's a type of staticky, *shhh* sound that has equal energy across all frequencies within the audible range. Pink noise has a slightly different sound profile and is often described as resembling the sound of rainfall or a waterfall. The powerful lower frequencies of brown noise offer a deeper, rumbling sound.

You can find free binaural beats, as well as white, brown, and pink noise tracks, available for free on YouTube, Spotify, and other sleeping platforms. Search for "Binaural Beats for Relax-

---

18. Aghajan et al., "Theta Oscillations in the Human Medial Temporal Lobe."

ation" or your noise of choice on your preferred streaming platform, and create a playlist for yourself with a few tracks. Try these different sound profiles on for size to see what works for you. With time and dedication, you will learn how to develop healthy sleep rituals that work for you. Remember that it's a process, and progress may be gradual. Stay committed to your plan, be patient with yourself, and trust that with consistency, you can improve your sleep patterns and enjoy better quality sleep.

Chapter Reflections

Developing a better relationship with sleep is an ongoing journey. Check in with yourself as you work toward better sleep and overall well-being. These journaling prompts are designed to help you gain deeper insight into your sleep patterns, identify obstacles that may arise, and cultivate a more compassionate and patient attitude toward yourself. By reflecting on these prompts, you can explore how to create a soothing sleep environment, envision the impact of consistent rest on other areas of your life, and build strategies to overcome challenges that may arise along the way.

- In what ways can you create a soothing sleep environment to promote relaxation and enhance your sleep quality?
- What obstacles or challenges do you foresee when it comes to implementing these changes? How could you overcome them to create consistent, healthy sleep habits?
- How would the rest of your life change if you got consistent rest? How would your body feel, and how would your mind operate if you gave yourself a chance to restore?
- How will you practice patience with yourself on your journey to better sleep?

Chapter Summary

Healthy, deep sleep is a crucial element in managing anxiety, and creating better morning and evening routines is the first step toward improving overall sleep health. If you're struggling to achieve deep sleep at night, you can still receive the positive, restorative benefits of rest through napping and NSDR.

Implementation Break

Congratulations on completing part 1 of this book. Now, it's time to pause and take a well-deserved implementation break. During this break, allow yourself to integrate the knowledge and practices you've encountered. Take some time for self-care, engage in activities that bring you joy, and savor the sense of accomplishment that comes with self-discovery.

PART TWO

SOUL GUIDANCE AND EMOTIONAL HEALING

Chapter Four
BECOME SELF-ISH

B y now, you're equipped with plenty of tools and concepts that will accelerate your anxiety transformation. This part of the book will be bringing in more of the emotional and energetic components of the journey from anxiety to empowerment.

Before we dive into this chapter, I invite you to make a promise to yourself. Promise that you'll allow yourself to become a little bit more selfish. When I say "selfish," I don't mean it in the traditional sense of the word, like being inconsiderate or self-centered. What I'm actually suggesting is to become self-ish, to embody a state of being where your thoughts, decisions, and actions are grounded in your worth. Taking this step is vital because the journey to self-empowerment involves nurturing yourself emotionally and energetically. It's about acknowledging your worthiness and recognizing that you deserve to embrace the fullness of your true, beautiful, and amazing self. And in order to do that, you've got to create a little bit more time for your self.

The self-empowerment journey requires you to step up and claim (really, truly *claim*) your worthiness, and know (really, truly *know*) your enoughness. Empowerment requires you to take up space, be seen, be heard, and be loved. It asks you to raise the bar for how to treat yourself. It wants you to be proud of how far you've come and excited for where you'll go. It demands that you show up for yourself differently. If that feels a little scary, I have good news for you: you're already doing it. You're already on the journey just by reading this book. At this point, you have the tools to change your relationship with anxiety. Becoming self-ish is how you optimize your use of these tools, and it paves a smoother path to empowerment. You're ready to be self-ish.

The Anxiety of Self-ishness

When we hear the word *selfish*, it often carries a negative connotation. We might picture someone who only thinks about themselves, disregarding the needs and feelings of others. However, there's another way to think about being selfish, one that emphasizes the importance of taking care of oneself in order to show up for others in a more meaningful way. This kind of "selfishness" is not about being selfish at the expense of others, but rather about taking care of our own needs and well-being so that we can be the best version of ourselves and better serve those around us.

Anxious people often struggle with the idea of putting themselves first, even if it's desperately needed. For many, just thinking about self-prioritization induces anxiety, because they've spent way too long putting their own needs (i.e., their happiness, healing, and growth) on the back burner. If you have spent years of your life putting yourself last, it's understandable that flipping the script might feel scary—but "scary" isn't always synonymous with "bad." In this case, it's quite the opposite.

Becoming self-ish is a way of serving justice to the anxious part of your brain that has been fixated on your not-enoughness.

Anxious or doubtful about your ability to be loved? Self-ishly offer yourself copious, unending compassion and appreciation. Exhausted and overwhelmed by how much you give to others? Self-ishly start to set boundaries that will give you back space, time, and peace. Always worried about what other people think? Self-ishly start asking yourself what *you* think—and decide that your opinions are pretty damn important too.

If you're uncertain about what being self-ish entails, begin by observing how you "should" yourself. This process involves paying attention to your internal dialogue. Where are you imposing unrealistic expectations and pressures on yourself? Hint: these expectations often lead to feelings of guilt or inadequacy. Notice moments when you find yourself thinking things like:

- *I should really answer that email before I go to bed.*
- *I should just go out with that person; I don't want to hurt their feelings.*
- *I should have more energy right now. I got a decent amount of sleep last night.*

These "should" statements might come from a place of self-criticism or the belief that you must meet certain external standards. Becoming aware of these thoughts is the first step in understanding how anxiety influences your perception of self and your actions. In many cases, "should" statements are the antithesis of self-ishness: by following "shoulds" like these, you might find yourself prioritizing others' needs and opinions over your own, giving away your power in the process.

Other times, your little "shoulds" are actually trying to point you toward the care you truly do need to give yourself. If this is the case, your should-ing may also show up with a tinge of guilt.

- *I know I should rest, but I need to get some more work done first.*
- *I should probably set a boundary with my coworkers because I'm overwhelmed at work. But if I don't handle things, who will?*
- *I should really stay in and have an early night, but if I don't go out, my friends will be mad at me.*

"Shoulds" like these arise from a conflict between your authentic needs and external expectations or obligations. When your "shoulds" carry a hint of guilt, it's a signal that you may not be fully honoring your own boundaries or self-care needs. This moment of reflection can become a turning point in embracing self-ishness.

Bottom line: start dealing with your resistance to self-care by inspecting your inner dialogue. It's bound to give you clues about where you...ahem, *should*...start being more self-ish.

Journaling Prompts to Identify Your Self-ish Needs

Take a moment to reflect on the following prompts.

- What does it mean for you to be self-ish?
- Does the idea of being self-ish scare you? Why or why not?
- Why is it important for you to be more self-ish on your empowerment journey?

Unlike a selfish person, who believes they are at the center of the universe, a self-ish person understands how to be a centered person within the universe. And as a centered person in this great, big universe, they know how important it is to prioritize their healing, their rest, their joy, and their growth. When you prioritize your own healing, you get to be the best version of yourself for everyone around you.

A Selfish Person...

- Lacks consideration for other people.
- Uses harmful language with others.
- Chooses to remain unaware of the impact they have on others.
- Is exclusively concerned with their own pleasure, success, and happiness, and is relentless in that pursuit.
- Is too focused on themselves to care for other people.

A Self-ish Person...

- Has consideration for others.
- Uses compassionate language with self and others.
- Has an awareness of their impact on others, and has healthy boundaries for themselves.
- Understands what contributes to their pleasure, success, and happiness, and does their best to create more of those experiences.
- Is connected to themselves and happily shows up for others with a full cup.

Notice how the traits of a selfish person include considerations about other people too. When you begin to really, truly step into your power, the people around you will benefit from this better version of yourself as well.

If the idea of focusing on yourself feels scary or wrong to you, you're not alone. While I believe society is making great improvements in this regard, it's still taboo to really dedicate time to focusing on yourself. If you're someone who has been conditioned to put yourself (and, thus, your healing) on the back burner, please know that choosing to be selfish is a sacred, empowered, and necessary act of rebellion, even if the thought of it makes you a little uncomfortable. It's okay if you feel resistant to this idea, or even a little anxious about it. Actually, feeling a little anxiety here is great, because it's lighting up an area that's worth exploring. So, let's explore!

Journaling Prompts to Explore Your Fears about Self-ishness

In your journal, write your answers to the following questions.

- What (or who) do you fear you will lose if you start taking up more space?
- What do you fear will fall apart, or what negative things do you believe might happen, if you become more self-ish?
- Do you have proof that any negative things will happen? If you don't have proof, why do you think your brain wants to create "proof"? Explain.
- What negative things might happen if you don't learn to be more self-ish?

Once you've finished your reflections, read through your answers again. You might choose to meditate on your reflections, or you can wrap up the exercise with a final journaling prompt.

- What are you learning about yourself and your needs through these reflections?

Selfishness and the Ego

When I'm working with clients on this subject, I commonly hear the same fear: "I'm afraid that if I pay too much attention to myself, I'll become a narcissist!" Be honest: did you have the same thought?

I empathize deeply when someone expresses such a fear, but I also find it a little bit humorous too—the fear of becoming a narcissist is such a paradox! A true narcissist, by definition, wouldn't be all that concerned with being seen as one. Those who are diagnosed with Narcissistic Personality Disorder are categorized, in part, by having little interest in self-reflection or ownership of shortcomings. If you're afraid of becoming a narcissist, chances are you're not one, and you will likely never become one.

I do understand that fear, though. I think it's born from a misunderstanding of the ego, and specifically the way we use the word *ego* in today's society. With the exception of a few communities (such as self-help and spirituality), "ego" has a pretty negative connotation. Usually, when someone is described as "having a huge ego," it's not meant as a compliment; it's a nicer way of saying, "Yeah, that person is a real a-hole."

Understandably, most people (especially anxious people) don't want to be seen as having an ego. But the way we use "ego" today is a bit of a departure from the word's simple origins. *Ego* is just the Latin word for *I*. Eventually the word made its way into English language, where we began using the word to describe the ability to perceive our own existence.

If you're reading this sentence, and you are aware that you're reading this sentence, congratulations! You have an ego. We all do. All the time. And the state of our ego can fluctuate. There are different ways of understanding the ego, but once of the simplest is to imagine it as a sliding scale, with three points: low, healthy, and high.

Low Ego

State: Self-minimization

Relationship to Power: Struggles to own their power

Inner Dialogue: Talks down to self, often through shame, blame, doubt, or judgment

Behaviors: Puts self last; fears that their own self-care will upset or cause harm to others; afraid to take up space or be seen by others; self-worth is deeply affected by other people's feelings or opinions; may have poor boundaries with others; tends to believe negative stories about self; lacks trust in self and may have disordered level of trust in others

Other Traits: Insecure; lacks confidence; lacks healthy awareness of self

Manifests As: Burnout, people-pleasing, apathy, sadness, or avoidance

If the Ego Could Talk, It Would Say: "Everyone else shines brighter than me."

Healthy Ego

State: Self-empowerment

Relationship to Power: Embraces their power

Inner Dialogue: Loving and compassionate with self; forgiving and supportive

Behaviors: Puts self first; embraces self-care and understand that self-care allows them to show up for others in a healthy way; takes up space, but makes room for others; is able to separate the emotions and opinions of other people from their own; understands how to separate truth-based thoughts from negative stories; creates healthy boundaries; is honest and compassionate, both with self and others; has a healthy trust in self and others

Other Traits: Secure; confident; aware of self

Manifests As: Joy, creativity, rest, or self-reflection

If the Ego Could Talk, It Would Say: "When I shine, you shine."

High Ego

State: Self-righteousness

Relationship to Power: Fixated on their power

Inner Dialogue: Aggrandizes self; feeds their worth by putting down others

Behaviors: Puts self on a pedestal; solely focuses on meeting own needs; takes up all the space, leaving no room for others; does not consider others' emotions or opinions at all; manipulative; enforces their perspectives to gain control over other people and circumstances; creates their own "truths" by telling stories that serve their ego; dishonest with self; accrues trust in self by successfully gaining power over others

Other Traits: Cocky; selfish; exaggerated obsession with self

Manifests As: Power, control, or self-obsession

If the Ego Could Talk, It Would Say: "I am the sun, and I don't care if my shine blinds others."

We all have ego. It's an ever-changing state of consciousness, and it's only human to fluctuate between low and high ego. What matters most is your commitment to creating a healthy ego, and remembering to returning to it when you're stuck in one of the extremes for too long.

Journaling on the States of the Ego

The following prompts will help you better understand how you relate to your own ego.

- What does it look and feel like when you show up with low ego? High ego? Healthy ego? Explain, and give an example for each.
- What ego state do you feel most comfortable in, and why?
- Is that a good or a bad thing? Explain.

Once you've completed those reflections, it's time to put some thought toward defining what healthy ego looks like for you.

- What would it be like, look like, and feel like for you to be in a state of healthy ego?
- What would be required from you to maintain a state of healthy ego?
- How would you prioritize your happiness, your healing, and your growth?
- What part(s) of your life would be positively impacted if you consistently showed up with a healthy ego?
- How would healthy ego grant you permission to be wonderfully, delightfully self-ish? Would you want to be more self-ish about your rest? About the quality of your thoughts?

About the people in your life? About the way you use (or give away) your energy?

And then, the most important journaling question of all:

- Can you start now?

Start Now

You can. I guarantee you can. Even if you're only warming up to the idea of self-ishness, even if you can "only" introduce a few, small acts of healthy ego right now—that is still a start. Small, accessible changes that are reinforced over time create the perfect recipe for change that withstands the test of time.

You might also consider bolstering that healthy ego of yours with some fun self-love tools. Here are a few of my favorites.

EXERCISE
Mirror Work for Self-ishness
🦋

Do this each morning for one week straight while you brush your teeth.

1. Look at yourself in the mirror, and stare directly into your own eyes.
2. Hold that gaze. If it's uncomfortable, ask yourself why (but don't dwell on the answer).
3. Repeat—out loud—the following: "I am proud of who you were yesterday, who you are today, and who you will become tomorrow. I love you. I forgive you, and I am here with you."

Mirror work can be a challenging practice, as it requires facing yourself in a very direct way. It can bring up feelings of discomfort or vulnerability, but those feelings are a sign that you're touching on important work. Lean in to the discomfort. Be okay with it feeling uncomfortable, cheesy, or awkward at first; a part of the work here is learning to feel comfortable taking up space and truly seeing yourself.

EXERCISE
Healthy Ego Scheduling

If you're someone who wants to make time for themselves, but you struggle with setting boundaries around your time, schedule your self-ishness into your calendar. If you have a busy life, setting a general intention like "I need to find time to relax this week" isn't going to cut it. You've got to be specific and intentional about when you're going to take time for yourself.

- **Start by identifying an area in your life where you'd like to be little more self-ish.** As an example: "I want to be more self-ish about my free time after work. I'd really like to use that time to do things I want to do, like guilt-free decompression, or an evening job, or maybe I'll even read that book I bought six months ago."

- **Then, think about how your anxiety brain tries to convince you that you can't or don't deserve to enact your desired self-ishness.** For example: "I can't take time for myself. Someone always needs something from me. I feel bad if I just shut my door or turn my phone on silent. I'm afraid that if I unplug, someone will get mad at me, or I'll get in trouble with work, or something bad will happen."

- **Create a recurring event on your calendar to "hold" time for your self-ishness each week.** Yes, a recurring event— and hold that time as sacred. Add blocks of time on your calendar, whether it's thirty minutes or a few hours, and treat them as an important appointment with yourself. This may require saying no to some things or delegating tasks to others, but it's worth it to prioritize your own well-being. When you have dedicated time on your calendar, you'll be less likely to push off or deprioritize much-needed "you" time. And this way, no matter how busy or stressful the week gets, you can look forward to that appointment with yourself.

I remember one of my clients expressing how silly she felt for even needing to schedule her self-ishness. She felt like it was something she "should" already be doing, and she was frustrated that had to resort to adding solo time to her calendar. If you feel the same way, please understand that there is absolutely nothing to feel silly or shameful about. Life gets busy! The important thing is that you're taking the steps now to reintroduce sacred self-prioritization time.

EXERCISE
Practicing the Self-ish "No"

Learning to set healthy boundaries is an essential part of becoming self-ish, and "no" is one of the most powerful boundaries you can establish. Many anxious people struggle with saying no due to the fear of disappointing others or being judged for setting a boundary. Constantly saying yes to others (especially at the cost of your own emotional and physical well-being) will leave you feeling drained, resentful, and overwhelmed. By boosting your confidence to say "no," you regain control of your time, space, and energy. Sometimes a "no" to other people is a "yes" to yourself.

If you struggle to say no and set boundaries around your time, space, and energy, journal and reflect on the following prompts:

- **What are your needs and priorities?** Before you can start saying no to requests or invitations, you need to have a clear sense of what is important to you. Take some time to reflect on your values and priorities, such as your health, your relationships, your career, or your personal interests.

- **In order to respect your needs and priorities, where do you need to set better boundaries?** Once you have a sense of your values and priorities, get clear on why those needs go unmet. Are there particular people, places, or things in your life that you let override your emotional and energetic needs?

- **What specific boundaries do you need to set?** This might mean setting limits on how much work you take on, how many social events you attend, or how much time you spend on certain activities.

Once you've finished responding to those prompts, it's time to say no!

1. **Practice saying no.** Start small by saying no to small requests, or practice with people who you know will be understanding of your boundary. You can also script out

specific boundary-setting statements ahead of time to help you feel more confident in your communication.

2. **Use "I" statements.** When you communicate a self-ish no, use "I" statements to express your own needs and boundaries, which keeps the energy clean and clear. For example, you might say, "I'm sorry, but I can't take on that project right now. I have too much on my plate."

3. **After you've expressed the "no" to others, experience the "no" for yourself.** Hold, honor, and follow through on your "no." If you turned down a social invitation because you want to catch up on rest, actually let yourself rest. If you said no to a demanding coworker or family member, give yourself permission to feel proud of your progress.

4. **Reflect on your experience.** After practicing saying no, take some time to reflect on how it felt and how it impacted your overall well-being. Did it feel empowering or uncomfortable? Did it help you prioritize your own needs and values? Use this reflection to inform your future boundary-setting and decision-making.

Setting boundaries and saying no is not easy work! It can be uncomfortable, and it's natural to worry about disappointing others or being seen as the "bad kind" of selfish. But you've got to remember that you have a right to prioritize your own needs and well-being. Saying no doesn't make you a bad person—it's simply a way to ensure that you are not overextending yourself and that you have the time and energy to focus on the things that matter most to you.

Keep It Going

Self-ishness is about giving yourself permission to honor your own unique needs, values, and interests. It's about finding joy and fulfillment in your own life, and not just living to please others or meet their expectations. The exercises and reflections in this chapter are designed to give you a head start on embracing a little self-ishness, but I want you to build on this! Keep your eyes, mind, and heart open for opportunities where you can practice prioritizing your needs in a healthy and positive way.

When you take better care of yourself, you'll have more space to listen to the healing your soul is craving. Taking care of yourself is not selfish—it is an act of self-love and self-respect. By prioritizing your own needs and making time for self-care, you create more room to tune in to your inner voice and attend to the deeper needs of your soul. This is not only beneficial for you, but it also positively impacts those around you as you become more centered, grounded, and in tune with your true self. So, don't hesitate to take care of yourself, honor your boundaries, and make time for the things that bring you joy and peace. Remember, the more you nourish your mind, body, and soul, the more you will thrive and grow in all aspects of your life.

Chapter Reflections

Take a moment to celebrate your progress and growth, and recognize the positive steps you've taken so far. Acknowledge the self-ishness you've already embraced. Above all, remember that this is a lifelong journey.

- Consider moments in your life when you've noticed the influence of each ego state. How did each state manifest in your thoughts, emotions, and behaviors? Are there any recurring patterns or themes?

- Does the idea of embracing self-ishness resonate with you? How does it make you feel? Explore any emotions or resistance that may arise when considering this concept.

- Think about instances when you may have prioritized others' needs and emotions over your own. How did that impact your well-being and sense of self? Is there an area in your life where you could practice self-ishness in a positive way?

- Identify situations where you tend to fall into certain ego states more frequently. Are there any triggers or patterns that lead you into these states? How do you typically respond when in each state?

- Reflect on any limiting beliefs or self-critical thoughts that have held you back from embracing self-ishness. How can you challenge those beliefs and cultivate a more empowering mindset?

- Imagine your life with a stronger connection to your self-ishness. How might your relationships, self-care, and overall well-being improve? What steps can you take to move closer to this state?

- Consider times when you've found it challenging to prioritize your own needs and boundaries. How can you set healthier boundaries and communicate your needs more effectively in the future?

- Explore any fears or concerns about becoming more self-centered in a positive way. What strategies can you employ to address these fears and move forward with confidence?

Chapter Summary

Self-ishness is not about being self-centered or inconsiderate of others—it is a profound act of self-love and a testament to the value you place on your well-being. Embracing self-ishness means recognizing that tending to your needs and desires is not only acceptable, but *essential* for your overall growth and flourishing. In a world that often emphasizes self-sacrifice and putting others first, this chapter celebrates the empowering practice of prioritizing yourself. By giving yourself permission to be self-ish, you grant yourself the time to heal, grow, and become the best version of yourself.

Chapter Five
DIALOGUE WITH THE SOUL

After building a toolkit of practices to address physical anxiety, the next logical step would be for us to build on that work and explore how to rewire anxious thoughts and behaviors—but we're not going to do that just yet, because anxiety isn't logical. Anxiety is emotional. By understanding and working through emotional responses first, we can create a stronger foundation to effectively rewire anxious thoughts and behaviors later on.

Traditional neural reprogramming (the practice of retraining your mind to connect with new, unanxious belief systems) can be summarized as taking a "think and feel" approach: think a new thought and, eventually, you will feel the truth of it. As someone who has studied and practiced neural reprogramming for years, I sincerely believe this approach has merit—but as someone who also lived with a deeply anxious mind, the simple practice of "thinking and feeling" isn't always so simple.

Perhaps you've tried the "think and feel" approach with your own anxiety in the past; you wanted to retrain your mind to think more positively, but your replacement thoughts didn't yield the long-term, embodied change you were hoping for.

When positive inner dialogue changes aren't sticking, it's because there are deeper emotional wounds that still need tending to. There's a part of the psyche, however small, that can't yet fully accept or believe the new, positive thoughts that are being practiced. That tender, unhealed corner of the mind isn't something that can just be affirmed away until the wounding disappears. It has to be healed. When unhealed belief systems go untended to, they will continue to interfere with the attempts to rewire and truly embody new belief systems.

Instead of "think and feel," I invite you to explore an alternative approach: "heal and feel."

The Spiritual Side of Anxiety: A Call from Your Soul to Heal

This is where the spiritual aspect of anxiety begins to come forward: the soul is calling out to heal the parts of the psyche that aren't yet able to accept and embody a more loving and empowered concept of self.

Anxious thoughts simply cannot be addressed in the mind alone. Authentic, positive change requires *all* parts of you: mind, body, and soul. That's why I believe it's so important to start with addressing the anxiety spin cycle: when you learn to dial down the anxious noise in your brain and body, it's easier to listen to the call from your soul.

If you have trouble wrapping your head around the concept of what a soul is, think about it like this: your soul is that core, immaterial part of you that is pure love. The part of you that has always, always known you to be whole. Healed. Healthy. Worthy. Enough.

The trouble with being human, of course, is that the anxiety brain works overtime to get us to forget about all of that. We forget our wholeness and replace it with judgment about the past, fear of the future, and negative stories about ourselves in the present. But no matter how deeply entangled you are in your anxious thoughts, there is always a way to untangle yourself from them too. Because the soul (the part of you that remembers how worthy and whole and enough you already are) hasn't gone anywhere. In fact, that's usually when your soul is trying the hardest to get your attention, and it's using your anxiety as a cue: it's time to release something, to heal something, or to transform something. This is your soul work.

Dialoguing with the Soul

It might already be clear to you what "soul work" is at the core of your anxiety. Some people will center in on a general core narrative that needs healing, like "My anxiety is asking me to improve my self-worth." Others may realize their work is more nuanced: "I have to heal from a specific trauma that has impacted the way I interact with the world around me." Everyone's work is different, and the best way to understand what's at the core of your anxiety is to dialogue directly with your soul.

You're actually in constant dialogue with your soul. Or, at least, your soul is in constant dialogue with *you*. But because we're human, that line of communication between the active, thinking mind and the wisdom of the soul can get pretty noisy. The following exercises serve as tools to help you reconnect with the wisdom that already lies within you. They will help you gain clarity on your deeper soul work.

EXERCISE
Soul Guidance Meditation

This is a self-guided meditation. Before beginning, read through the description in full to familiarize yourself with the direction of your meditation. You may want to have a journal handy to take notes or capture any thoughts that come up. Remember, this practice is less about thinking and more about receiving; you don't have to make sense of any insights, figure out any messages, or "fix" anything in this moment.

1. Find a comfortable seat in a chair, with your spine upright and shoulders soft. Feel both feet planted firmly on the ground. Place your right palm on your thigh to connect with your body. Place your left hand on your thigh, palm facing up, energetically opening yourself to receiving insight.

2. Begin to take deep, calm, easy breaths in and out through the nose. Give yourself a few cycles of deep breathing to simply connect with your body. Notice any spaces in the physical body that feel tight, stuck, or like they're holding on to something.

3. In your mind's eye, locate the base of your spine. Begin to envision a cord of white light dropping down from the base of your spine. See the cord connecting with the core of the earth, just like a ship dropping an anchor into the center of the ocean. Feel the effects of gravity and allow your body to truly become grounded in your space.

4. Then, begin to envision another cord of white light extending down from the cosmos and connecting to

the crown of your head. Allow both lines of energy to connect in the center of your body. Breathe and feel. Allow this cord of white light to begin radiating outward, enveloping your physical body in a bubble.

5. Bring your attention to the center of your head, in the space right behind your eyes. Allow your awareness to rest here.

6. In your mind's eye, imagine a radio dial or a knob in front of you, and label it as your "intellectualizer." Your intellectualizer is the part of your being that rationalizes, compartmentalizes, or minimizes your inner wisdom.

7. Turn down the knob of your intellectualizer. Notice how far you are able to turn it down. Can you get it to zero? Does your intellectualizer want to remain turned on to about 10 or 15 percent? There is no right or wrong here; just notice what you notice.

8. With your intellectualizer turned down, begin to rest your awareness in your heart's center.

9. Say hello to your inner wisdom. Say hello to your soul. Invite their guidance and wisdom into your meditation practice. Spend a few minutes breathing, feeling, and noticing how your body responds when you open up the line of communication with your inner wisdom. Notice if strong emotions come forward. You may experience chills, tears, joy, or another visceral experience; allow what comes up to simply be without labeling it as "good" or "bad."

10. Then, spend a few minutes reflecting on any of the following questions.

- What does your soul want you to understand about your anxiety?

- What is the deeper healing work you are being called to?
- How can you be more compassionate and loving toward yourself on this journey?

When you feel complete, take a few deep breaths and open your eyes.

EXERCISE
Automatic Writing

Automatic writing is one of my favorite ways to get out of the monkey mind and start dialoguing with the soul. It's a practice that allows you to tune in to a deeper level of consciousness—in this case, the guidance of your own soul. Your pen will do the talking as you begin to write freely. It should feel, well, automatic. As if the words are pouring straight out of the heart, not the brain. You'll feel when the anxiety brain wants to turn "on" and begin to do the writing for you: it's usually when your train of thought breaks, or you second-guess the words you're putting down on the paper. If that happens, don't sweat it. Just take a few deep breaths, release, and reconnect to your inner knowing.

For this exercise, choose a day where you're able to set aside thirty minutes or more. If possible, aim for first thing in the morning or right before bed. Find or create a sacred space to do this exercise. You don't have to run out and buy a bunch of fancy-schmancy "spiritual" things to decorate your room with, but I do encourage you to find a way to make the space you choose to reflect in feel special. Ask yourself, *What feels sacred to me? How can I create a space that feels inviting?* You might choose to light candles, play soothing music, or set up a bunch of cozy pillows to lie on. Make sure to wear comfortable clothes, and have water and your journal handy.

1. Grab your journal, find a comfortable spot to sit, and drop into your body with a few cycles of deep breathing. This is a great time to integrate heart-focused breathing or box breathing.

2. Ground your energy. Close your eyes, and visualize a band of white light extending from the base of your spine deep into the earth. Then, "see" a second band of white light pouring down from the sky and connecting with the crown of your head. Allow those two streams of light to meet in the center of your body. Keep breathing, and visualize that light enveloping your entire body. This is your sacred space, where you will listen for the calls from your soul.

3. Call upon the wisdom of your soul with the following invocation: "I now open myself up to receive, feel, and know the wisdom of my soul. Allow me to receive all that comes through, in service of my highest and best good, and the good of all others around me, both known and unknown."

4. Breathe deeply, open your eyes, and begin to automatically write on any (or all) of the following questions.

- When it comes to your anxiety, what does your soul want you to understand?

- What "soul work" is trying to reach you? What is at the core of your anxiety? What is asking to be witnessed, released, or healed?

- What have you been doing to block your own path to healing?
- What can you do to support your path to healing?

5. When you feel complete with the insight you've received, close your eyes, take a few deep breaths, and find a moment of gratitude for yourself. Close your journal to end the automatic writing practice.

Processing the Messages

It can be helpful to follow up on a spiritual reflection practice (like this one) with some additional writing prompts. Think of it as a way for you to better integrate the information that came through into real life. Here are my favorite processing questions to reflect on.

- **"I just learned…"** Zoom out from your practice. Was there anything else you learned about yourself that you'd like to document?
- **"Physically, I'm feeling…"** How does your body feel? Do you need water, a walk, some rest? Check in with yourself, and act on what comes up here.
- **"Emotionally, I'm feeling…"** How are you *actually* feeling? Excited? Intimidated? Happy? Fearful? There's no wrong answer here—you're just creating a touchpoint with yourself. Understanding how you feel is important, and it can help you better care for yourself throughout your journey.
- **"Based on this practice, one small next step I can integrate this week is…."** This is where you empower yourself! What is one small, manageable step you can take to continue your healing?

Emotional De-Layering

Sometimes, getting to the core of your soul work takes a bit of effort! Another helpful self-inquiry (or, in this case, soul inquiry) tool is something I like to call "emotional de-layering." Emotional de-layering is exactly what it sounds like: a simple framework for peeling back the layers of your emotions until you're able to better articulate or understand them. In the context of dialoguing with the soul, emotional de-layering is especially helpful if you're feeling super-fixated on your anxiety and are struggling to tune in to your inner guidance.

Practicing emotional de-layering is simple: whenever you feel "stuck" in an emotion or an experience, try to articulate as best you can what's bugging you. This is your "starter feeling" statement. Then, gently ask yourself questions like *Why?* or *What's underneath that?* or *Is that true?* as if you're having a conversation with an old friend. Really, you can use any short, simple questions that make sense in context and will coax some more honest feeling statements out of you. Keep asking short, simple questions to yourself until you get to your "core feeling." You'll know you've hit a core feeling when it connects to a negative belief system, and your soul work (or at least a piece of it) lies in the healing of it.

Here's a personal example from my days in the corporate world. I had come home from work in a self-described mood, which had become a trend after accepting my new job at a scrappy startup. It was the type of work environment where every employee wore multiple hats, and there were plenty of circumstantial reasons as to why I was feeling moody. I was running on less sleep than normal, my days were packed with meetings, and I had been spending most of my evenings at home preparing a presentation for an important new client. While it was a stressful period of time, there wasn't anything unconventional or new about this stress; I had worked at a handful of startups prior to taking this new job, and the stress I was experiencing was par for the course. I assumed that after the big presentation, I'd start to feel a little more relaxed again.

And yet, after the presentation was finally over, I noticed that I was still feeling anxious—even more so than I did before. When I wasn't able to get to the root of why I felt more anxious, I broke out my journal and began a de-layering writing process. Here are the questions I asked myself.

- **What is my feeling statement?** "I'm feeling a weird mix of anger and exhaustion and just want to quit my job."

- **Why am I feeling that way?** "Because today sucked."

- **What's underneath that?** "I worked really hard on a presentation, and nobody said anything about it. Now I feel like I did a bad job."

- **Is that feeling true, or is it a story? Do I actually believe I did a bad job?** "Well, not entirely. I actually thought I did a pretty great job on the presentation. I felt really proud of my work."

- **What's really underneath me feeling upset today?** "I didn't get the validation I wanted, and I let it affect my entire mood."

- **Why?** "I'm not sure why it affects me so much, but it's really hard for me to not base my own mood on how other people are responding to me. Now that I'm thinking about it, this doesn't just happen at work. My anxiety can get triggered if I feel like my friends or family don't verbally appreciate the work I've done. When I don't get that validation, I start to feel like there's no point in doing anything."

- **What is the core negative feeling?** "I'm realizing that there is a big part of me that only feels worthy if I get that validation from other people."

In the process of de-layering my anxiety, I discovered a profound truth about myself: a significant part of my self-worth and self-perception was deeply entwined with seeking validation from others. Whenever I didn't receive the external validation I craved, especially in relation to my work, I'd spiral into worry, questioning whether I or my efforts were truly enough.

This newfound awareness became a pivotal aspect of my soul work, prompting me to embark on a journey of untangling my worth from others' opinions and praise. Initially, this soul work manifested in my career, but its impact extended far beyond that domain, touching every aspect of my life. The process of de-layering anxious feelings and recognizing their root cause became a catalyst for my transformation. I realized that true empowerment came from within, and I needed to embrace my inherent worth regardless of external validation.

WHAT HAPPENS IF THE MESSAGE IS "I DON'T KNOW"?

If you keep coming up with a resounding "I don't know" when you reflect on what your soul work is, don't worry! It's not uncommon for "I don't know" to be the first (or only) thought that pops into your mind. In many cases, it's a safety response: it's easier for the brain to render an automatic "I don't know" than it is to go into deep reflection, especially if that reflection is going to dig up some tender topics. As the saying goes, "You can't heal what you don't reveal," so let's talk about how to get out of your "I don't know" and into your soul work.

First, have a little patience—and a lot more faith in yourself. Sometimes, the most appropriate answer to "What's my deeper soul work?" is "I don't know—yet. But I'm here, I'm open, and I'm patiently listening for the answer." Then, listen. Patiently. Stay open. Can you trust that your healing work will reveal itself to you when you're ready?

Sometimes, you do already know what your soul work is, and it's just a matter of asking different questions to find the answer. When I'm working with a client and their automatic response is an emphatic "Amanda, I have no idea what my anxiety is here for!" I'll say, "Great! You don't have to. But what if you had to take a guess?" Guessing is a fun little way of circumventing our subconscious fear of failure; most humans perceive guessing as having less "risk" of being wrong. Another sneaky question I like to ask is, "What if you *did* know the answer?" (This is always a fun one, because usually, the answer that comes up is exactly right!)

Now, there are a few cases where "I don't know" is an extremely valid answer. The brain has a unique ability to hide particularly stressful, fearful, or traumatic events as a means of protection. If you've experienced deep trauma and the brain has determined the emotional pain is too much to handle, accessing those memories may be challenging. For example, let's say an individual has severe anxiety around trusting others due to a traumatic incident that occurred in early childhood. If the brain has tucked that core memory away or deemed it too unsafe to unpack, it might be genuinely challenging for that person to reflect on the root of their anxiety.

I want to be clear here: the work in this book is about healing and feeling better. It is not about pushing yourself to explore or unpack something before you're ready. Be gentle with yourself as you reflect on your healing, especially if you are addressing a core trauma for the first time. Go slow, don't push past your capacity, and, whenever possible, ensure you are adequately resourced: do not be afraid to find additional support in the form of a therapist, counselor, coach, or other trauma-informed professional. Your deeper healing can benefit greatly from outside support that runs in parallel with this material. For example, if your soul work is calling you to heal a core belief about your ability to receive love, it may be beneficial to explore any wounding from early child-hood or adolescence with a professional. That healing will support you as you continue forward with the transformative work in this book.

Let Your Soul Guide Your Goal

The healing work that your soul inquiry reveals is your North Star. It's what you've got to remain connected to when you're improving your inner dialogue, rewiring your thoughts, and letting go of anxiety-driven patterns. Not only does your soul guidance serve as the framing for how you heal, it also lights up the pathway for *why* you heal: because there is an incredible, beautiful, empowered version of life waiting for you on the other side of your transformation.

After all, that's a part of the reason you picked up this book, right? You're here to transform your anxiety into empowerment. It's time to create change and commit to your transformation fully. In the next few chapters, we'll take a deep dive into understanding your triggers, rewiring your thoughts, changing your behaviors, and stepping into your empowered self.

Chapter Reflections

The next time you're having an anxious thought or feeling, practice emotional de-layering by writing in your journal or talking aloud to yourself in a voice memo. Additionally, use the following prompts to explore the concept of soul work to identify your unique healing path.

- What resonates with you the most when you think about the idea of "soul work" in relation to your anxiety journey?
- Have you experienced moments in your life where you sensed an underlying narrative impacting your anxiety? If so, what might that narrative be?
- How do you currently perceive the communication between your active mind and your soul? Is there room for improvement in this dialogue?
- Are there any recurring patterns or themes in your anxiety experiences that might point toward areas of soul work that require attention and healing?
- Have you ever felt a strong intuitive pull toward specific healing or growth in your life? How can you honor and explore these instincts further?

Chapter Summary

Your soul is calling out to you to heal. You can tune in and listen to that call through soul dialogue and conscious reflection in your journal. Remember, your soul is a compassionate guide that's gently nudging you toward your own unique path to healing. Listening to this call is an act of courage and vulnerability, a willingness to confront the shadows and embrace the light that resides within. Allow yourself the grace to listen, for in doing so, you'll find the wisdom to navigate your journey with newfound clarity and purpose. Trust in the wisdom of your soul.

Chapter Six
OWN YOUR AVOIDANCE

As humans, we love to mask anxiety in other behaviors. We'll busy ourselves with household tasks, bury ourselves in work, or take out some of our excess emotions on the people around us—anything to avoid the fact that we're triggered. Addressing avoidant tendencies is a necessary, yet uncomfortable, part of the empowerment journey. Your transformation requires you to take responsibility for the ways in which you self-sabotage or delay your healing.

We all have avoidant tendencies. Some people like to blow off steam with a bottle of wine; some indulge in a five-hour Netflix binge; others might doom-scroll on their phones until 2:00 a.m. Not only do these distraction tools provide a temporary escape from anxiety, they offer a major dopamine hit as well. Dopamine, the neurotransmitter often referred to as the "feel-good" chemical, plays a significant role in our brain's reward system. When we engage in activities that provide instant gratification or excitement, like scrolling through social media feeds or watching captivating videos, our brain releases dopamine.[19] This creates a feedback loop where we become conditioned to seek out these

19. Haynes, "Dopamine, Smartphones & You."

distractions whenever we feel anxious or stressed. The momentary pleasure experienced while engaging in these activities often quiets underlying emotions and temporarily alleviates feelings of discomfort.

However, this relief is short-lived. When someone is engaging in avoidance, anxious feelings may temporarily subside, but that person is really just experiencing a false sense of comfort. Numbing out and distracting the mind robs us of the opportunity to address the underlying cause of anxiety. Instead of confronting the root of the issue, it's merely put on hold, which means the issue is still simmering beneath the surface. As that temporary relief fades, anxiety often comes rushing back even stronger. It's like putting a bandage on a wound that requires stitches. Distractions don't make anxiety disappear—they just keep uncomfortable emotions at bay for a little while.

To break free from this cycle, addressing avoidant behaviors is essential. It's crucial to take responsibility for any self-sabotaging tendencies or actions that hinder healing. Being honest with yourself, identifying personal blocks, and making healthier choices from that point on are key steps toward progress.

The trickiest aspect of addressing avoidance is recognizing its presence. For many people, avoidant behaviors have become so ingrained that they go unnoticed or don't raise any red flags. That was certainly the case for me; I only became aware of my avoidant tendencies when my mental health bottomed out. My self-worth was six feet under, my relationships were a mess, and I had adopted the "work hard, party hard" mentality: every sixty-hour workweek was "rewarded" with binge drinking as my only outlet for release. I never stopped to actually think about what my true needs were (at the very least: rest, therapy, and a long cry). Instead, I would either act out or blackout, whichever happened first—anything to keep me in my pattern of avoidance. It was self-abandonment at its finest. It wasn't fun, but it was familiar. Unsurprisingly, my body would force-quit on me after a few weeks of consistent self-abandonment. It always started the same way: I'd wake up one morning with a cold. I'd tell myself I should just work from home for a few hours. Maybe I'd even order some takeout. *A nice little treat, and then I'm back to the grind*, I'd lie to myself. Without fail, "working from home" became more of an abstract concept than an actual expectation, and a "few hours" in bed would devolve into a few *days* in bed. When I'd enter one of those shutdowns, it wasn't uncommon for me to have an overwhelming number of missed calls and unanswered text messages at any given time. (I promise you, it was not because I was cool, mysterious, and popular. It was because I didn't have the energy to communicate with other people.)

I engaged that shutdown cycle for years, and it begs the question: how did I not see that I was in so much avoidance? A part of me just didn't understand how my partying and overworking were distracting me from healing. But, deep down, another part of me did recognize I was in avoidance. I just didn't want to look at it, so I stayed in that avoidant cycle for a while. I felt bad enough already, and I didn't need more reasons to judge myself! Eventually, I grew sick of the cycle and decided it was time to take ownership of my negative habits. In doing so, I started to realize that ownership work isn't supposed to be an act of self-judgment— it's an act of self-love. Examining the ways you distract yourself, numb out, or avoid dealing with things is one of the most responsible things you can do for your growth.

Avoiding feeling the emotions connected to your anxiety is a form of self-sabotage. Rather than facing the uncomfortable emotions and working through them, you're distracting yourself from the discomfort and extending your pain. This may provide temporary relief, but in the long run, it only perpetuates the anxiety and prevents you from truly healing and growing. By consistently avoiding your emotions, you'll miss out on the important messages they are trying to convey to you. Ultimately, those uncomfortable emotions you're avoiding are signals trying to show you that there are things in your life that are asking to be seen and healed. When you ignore these messages, you deprive yourself of the opportunity to live a more fulfilling and authentic life.

The work outlined in chapter 5 should have started to paint a picture of how your own avoidance manifests. As you work through this chapter, you'll crystallize that awareness, take ownership of your avoidance, and pave a path toward tangible change.

How Do You Avoid?

When you're activated, are you a shut-down-and-shut-out kind of person? A yeller? A crier? Perhaps you're a masker: someone who is great at pretending they're not anxious, only to come home and numb out with food, TV, alcohol, or drugs. There are hundreds, if not thousands, of potential avoidance tactics. These tactics range from emotional avoidance (like slowly shutting people out) to more in-your-face behavioral avoidance (like bingeing reality TV for days on end).

EMOTIONAL AVOIDANCE

Emotional avoidance habits are the things you do that starve yourself of the things you need: shutting down communication with loved ones due to shame, though you're desperately seeking connection; offering a smile and an "I'm fine" when all you want to do is scream about how not fine you are; being overwhelmed with work, but refusing help so as to not seem weak.

One time, when I was in one of my worst shutdown cycles, a friend came to my apartment unannounced to try and get me out of bed. I saw her texts and missed calls, I heard her knocking just feet away from where I was lying, and I still couldn't do it. Oprah Winfrey could have been texting me, begging to give me a million dollars, and I still wouldn't have answered. I just didn't have it in me. Pushing away connection was emblematic of my shutdowns, though ironically, a connection was perhaps what I needed most at that time. On a soul level, I was craving joy, purpose, and a sense of self. Still, I was in such a deep state of disconnect that I was rendered unconscious to any of my actual emotional needs. Because I hadn't stopped to examine these behaviors, I simply wasn't conscious of the fact that I was in avoidance. Sure, I could see that I wasn't awesome at taking care of myself, but I didn't understand it was avoidance until this particular friend and I finally hung out, and she voiced her concern.

My friend's compassionate approach was a wake-up call for me. Despite my attempts to avoid everyone, she didn't meet me with anger or confrontation. Instead, she showed me love and genuine concern. In a gentle manner, she pointed out my reclusiveness and decreased responsiveness over the past few months, prompting me to reflect on how I had been feeling lately. Hearing her concern for me was another aha moment: part of the reason I kept avoiding people was because I assumed they were already mad at me for being reclusive anyway. It snowballed from there, and my fear of judgment and rejection only fueled my emotional avoidance further. Knowing that she, along with our other friends, cared about my well-being, served as a powerful inspiration for me to start addressing my emotional avoidance.

When I finally mustered up the courage to take ownership of my avoidance, clarity came pouring in. Of course I had been in an endless loop of anxiety for so long! My time was spent on distractions, which weren't creating any room for me to just be, breathe, feel my feelings, and heal.

BEHAVIORAL AVOIDANCE

Behavioral avoidance is engaging in a tangible, unhealthy distraction. Often, behavioral avoidance involves a tool or an object outside of yourself to engage with. You might avoid by reaching for something (like your phone, a substance, work, food) or someone.

Owning behavioral avoidance isn't about getting rid of the things you used to avoid. In most cases, the tools themselves are neutral. There's nothing inherently wrong with checking social media or enjoying your favorite TV show or buying yourself some candy. It's the way in which you engage with the tools that constitutes avoidance: are you enjoying, or are you numbing? Are you honoring your boundaries, or are you engaging in excess? Is it replenishing you in some way, or is it filling a hole in you? Only you will be able to determine that.

The Journey of Avoidance

Owning your avoidance is a nonlinear journey. As an example, let's look at my client Saul. Saul's main form of emotional avoidance was to bury himself in his work. As a successful small business owner, Saul had plenty of good reasons as to why he was always working, and when taken at face value, his reasonings were valid! After all, entrepreneurship is an incredibly demanding and time-consuming endeavor, and Saul was genuinely passionate about his work. However, he and I both knew that he was using his work as a distraction from dealing with his years-long cycle of relationship anxiety and emotional avoidance.

As much as Saul wanted a partner, he had a pattern of jumping ship after a few months of dating someone. His workload would conveniently become extra busy every time one of his romantic relationships was becoming extra close. Saul would rationalize that he just wasn't able to balance his work and a relationship, but deep down, he knew that his overbooked schedule was his way to avoid dealing with his relationship anxiety and fear of emotional intimacy.

Eventually, Saul's avoidance habits started taking a toll on his physical and mental health. He was experiencing chronic stress, burnout, and even physical symptoms like headaches and stomach issues. Late work nights led to poor sleep, and he grew increasingly more irritable, reclusive, and burnt out. It was only after one final, heart-wrenching breakup that Saul finally decided it was time to address the cycle.

Saul and I spent about five months working together on his healing. We started by using the emotional de-layering method (from chapter 5) to uncover the heart of the matter. His starter feeling statement was "I just don't feel like I can balance work and a relationship at the same time." Saul was able to de-layer this statement to another feeling: "Relationships always take a lot of work, and my schedule is just too busy to accommodate the time for a relationship."

When taken at face value, the feeling Saul initially expressed here is completely valid. Relationships indeed take work, and there's nothing wrong with consciously choosing to prioritize your career over a relationship. For Saul, however, there was a part of him that deeply wanted a relationship, and this particular sentiment was his way of creating excuses and reengaging in his cycle of avoidance and self-sabotage. So, we de-layered some more. I asked him if it was true that he was really too busy for a relationship, and he admitted that, no, that wasn't entirely true. Saul realized that he had been subconsciously choosing to fill up his schedule so that he had an excuse to not date seriously.

This was progress, and I was eager to get Saul to de-layer that awareness just one more time. I asked him why he avoided dating seriously. He sat in silent reflection for a few minutes. Eventually, he cleared his throat and vulnerably shared, "I avoid relationships because I'm so afraid of failing at them. If I really show up for a person, and I fail, what does that say about me?"

This was an enormous breakthrough moment. Of course, deep down, Saul already knew all of this, but it was critical for him to be able to vocalize his patterns and call them out directly. By giving voice to patterns and acknowledging their presence, one can bring them out from the depths of the subconscious into the light of conscious awareness. This act of verbal, vulnerable acknowledgment opens the door to self-understanding, and it allows one to confront their patterns head-on.

At the core of Saul's avoidance, he actually held deep anxiety about relationships. He played it cool by staying busy and not getting too close to others, but these avoidant patterns were just temporary shields against his inner fear of not being enough. With this awareness now out in the open, Saul and I agreed that his ultimate "soul work" was to focus on developing his emotional vulnerability, self-love, and self-trust. We spent months working toward these healing goals together: during our sessions, we explored the root cause of his fear of vulnerability, practiced tools that would help him to stay present when he wanted to numb out, and even cleared up his schedule so that he couldn't lean on his excuse of being "too busy." In between our sessions, I also gave Saul journaling prompts that were designed to help him explore his avoidance and maintain a sense of connection to his emotions. (At the end of this chapter, you'll get to explore some of the very same journaling prompts I worked on with Saul.)

Thanks to his commitment to self-reflection and growth, Saul was able to take ownership of his avoidant tendencies and begin his healing process. He gained clarity about how his avoidance manifested (work), what he was avoiding (healing his intimacy wounds), and what he was going to do about it (therapy and better boundary-setting with himself). But, even with his newfound awareness and a solid plan in place, it still took him a while to fully break his cycle of avoidance.

For the first few months, Saul would slip back into his old patterns, and when he did, he'd feel like a failure and beat himself up over it. Saul was not a failure. He's human! Slipping back into old patterns of avoidance is normal, if not expected. When someone has spent years of their life engaging in a particular emotional pattern, it's not going to be as simple as turning a switch off and never doing that thing again. After one has identified how they avoid their emotions, they're going to still engage in those behaviors for a while, and that's okay! It takes time to unlearn years-long emotional patterns, and it requires copious amounts of grace and self-compassion. Trust that as long as you're staying engaged with your emotions, the healing will occur.

Healing certainly happened for Saul, by the way. At the end of our coaching, Saul had decided to take a few months off from casual dating. Now that he had a better grasp on his emotions and healing path, he used the newfound free time in his schedule to actually spend time with himself. He spent time traveling and volunteering, and he even developed a zen meditation practice.

The more time he spent enjoying his own company, the more his inner dialogue and self-worth improved. After about a year of focusing strictly on himself, Saul trusted in his ability to stay present with his emotions more than ever, and he actually felt ready to share himself—and his emotions—with another person. I'm thrilled to report that eventually Saul wound up meeting a fantastic partner, and they're still together to this day.

The Judgment Monster

As someone learns how to truly own and heal their avoidant tendencies, they'll naturally have moments of frustration and self-judgment, just like Saul did. When that happens, practicing gentle inner dialogue and self-forgiveness becomes critical. Change takes time, patience, and a hell of a lot of self-compassion. For those who tend to judge or shame themselves, or expect perfection, the best work that can be done is to practice copious amounts of self-compassion. Ownership work is meant to be an act of self-love, not an act of self-judgment. No matter how loudly that Judgment Monster is knocking at that door, don't let it in.

Ownership work is not meant to be an exercise in looking at all of the ways in which someone sucks. Rather, it's a curious, loving exploration of the habits that prevent or delay someone from stepping into the most aligned, grounded version of themselves. This particular part of the work is ripe with possibility: what incredible, fulfilling things will take up the space that your avoidance once occupied? Instead of judging yourself harshly or beating yourself up for falling into old patterns, approach this work with kindness and understanding.

The ACED Framework

When you notice self-judgment starting, remember the acronym ACED.

- **Acknowledge the feelings.** Once you've noticed you're in avoidance, take a moment to acknowledge what you are feeling. Recognize that these feelings are valid, and it's okay to experience them.
- **Clear the shame.** Focus on what the "win" is. Did you catch that you were avoiding faster than you did the last time? Were you gentler with yourself?
- **Examine the trigger.** Take note of what happened to trigger the avoidance. You might find some useful information that can help you the next time you want to avoid.
- **Decide how you'll course correct.** So, you slipped up. What will you do next to help get back on track? Do you need some self-care, a positive distraction, a forgiveness meditation, or something else?

Feel It to Heal It

Becoming aware of avoidance is a big step, but awareness itself won't magically stop the cycle. You've got to give yourself permission to actually *feel* the feelings you've been running from. As the saying goes, "What you resist, persists." By trying to avoid negative emotions, you're *still* giving those feelings your power, which means you are inadvertently strengthening the hold those emotions have over you. The key is learning how to move from resistance of the emotion into validation and acceptance of the emotion. By accepting what you're feeling and allowing yourself to experience it fully, you can begin to process and release it.

This is what is often referred to as *shadow work*. Shadow work is the process of exploring and integrating the parts of ourselves that we have rejected, denied, or repressed because they are deemed too painful to experience, or appear unacceptable in some way. When you learn to integrate the shadow emotions that lie underneath your anxiety (like sadness, anger, and shame) into conscious awareness, you remove the power that the shadow has over you. The benefits of shadow work are profound, but it can certainly feel scary to start confronting the uncomfortable emotions you've been avoiding.

Imagine being alone in a dark cave, huddled over a small fire. You think you're alone in the cave, but unbeknownst to you, there is a tiny lizard seated beside you. As the light from the fire casts a shadow against the cave wall, you glance over your shoulder and see not just your own shadow, but also the shadow of an enormous monster! Fear seizes you, and you immediately shut your eyes, turn back to the fire, and hope the monster will go away. A part of you really, really wants to move around, or even search for the monster, but your mind is fraught with reasons why that's a bad idea. You decide that you're better off staying where you are, so you spend the night paralyzed by fear. Throughout the night, you remain frozen, imagining what terrible things the monster might do to you. If only you had kept your eyes open and examined your surroundings, you would have realized that there was no monster behind you at all—it was just the shadow of the harmless lizard. This anecdote illustrates that fear and resistance have a funny way of making the things we're scared of seem much bigger than they are. The emotions you're afraid of feeling may be as harmless as that little lizard; they seem too big or too scary to deal with, but the size of the shadow is a distortion. Turn your awareness to what you're afraid of, and shine some light on the uncomfortable emotions—what you find might not be as scary as it seemed.

My client Jackie expressed a common fear about facing her emotions: she was afraid of getting "stuck" in the shadow. All her life, Jackie had been applauded for being a caring and giving person, but it had always been at the cost of her own needs and emotions. This pattern of over-giving was an anxious response built in childhood, where she had taken on the role of emotional caregiver in her family without receiving the support she needed in return. While Jackie felt enormous amounts of anger about this as a child, she learned that when she was able to offer support to her parents and receive validation for it, the pain would temporarily go away. This pattern continued on into adulthood: she'd give to others, receive nothing back, and then give *more* in hopes of receiving temporary validation. Over-giving to others helped her to avoid her childhood anger and cope in her adult life—but the underlying anxiety of not being loved or accepted persisted.

I completely understood Jackie's fear of feeling her feelings: she had spent decades of her life pushing her anger down, and she had created a pretty decent life for herself in spite of the deeper pain. Jackie was afraid that if she actually allowed herself to feel angry, she'd wallow in the pain or get stuck in her anger forever. Why risk what she had built? But, the truth was, Jackie was merely surviving, not thriving, and the true "risk" was is in *not* feeling the feelings. Jackie *wanted* to thrive, and she recognized that in order to do so, she'd have to begin the process of feeling her feelings, however big or scary they seemed.

It's understandable if you, like Jackie, feel afraid of getting stuck in your shadow, but it's important to remember that allowing yourself to feel your emotions is *not* the same as being consumed by them. To be consumed by emotions means that the shadow is taking over and dominating one's thoughts and actions to the extent that they become overwhelming or difficult to control; it can result in a loss of perspective, irrational behavior, and the inability to focus on anything else.

Feeling and acknowledging your emotions doesn't mean you won't experience the intensity of those feelings; you *will* experience the challenge that comes along with big feelings. But the way in which you respond to and listen to those big feelings is different: you'll learn to meet yourself in those feelings without judgment, and to do so in a way that allows for more compassion, self-nurturing, and understanding. You won't be stuck in the shadow forever if you learn to respond to the emotions differently. Emotions are fluid and meant to change, and by allowing yourself to feel them, you will move through them and eventually come to a place of greater peace and acceptance.

The "Feel Your Feelings" Framework

Here's the framework that Jackie and many of my other clients used to begin the process of feeling the feelings that they had been avoiding.

1. **Acknowledge your avoidant patterns.** Great news! By this point in the chapter, you've already got this step down.

2. **Recognize what avoidance feels like in your body.** Pay attention to the physical sensations you experience when you know you're running from something. Do you feel tight? Tense? Out of body? Observing your physical cues will help you catch yourself the next time you want to avoid a feeling.

3. **The next time you feel your avoidance creeping in, pause.** Once you've recognized that you're in avoidance, consciously pause and take a few deep breaths. Don't try to judge, analyze, or change how you're feeling—just sit in those feelings.

4. **Then, try to identify the emotion underneath the avoidance.** You may already know what you're feeling, but it's important to call it out: "I am sad." "I am angry." "I am scared."

5. **Sit with that emotion.** This is the uncomfortable part: you've got to let yourself be in the feeling. You've got to actually feel it. If you're sad, let yourself be sad. If you're angry, give yourself permission to scream into a pillow.

6. **Practice nonjudgment with the emotion.** Feel the emotion deeply, but don't label what you're feeling as "good" or "bad." Experiencing shadow emotions such as sadness, fear, or anger isn't an inherently bad thing—it's a natural part of the human experience.

7. **Explore the emotion.** Ask yourself questions about the emotion, such as *What triggered this feeling?* or *How long have I been keeping this in for?* There is valuable information to uncover within uncomfortable feelings. Use your journal to capture your reflections.

8. **Create a "landing pad" for yourself afterward.** Feeling your feelings is big work, and it's important that you continue care for yourself after you've explored an emotion. Drink some water, give your heart space a little rub, and shift into a soothing activity that can help you decompress.

The Power of Inner Child Work

Inner child work is a form of emotional processing that helps you connect with and heal the pain from early life that is influencing your emotions and choices in adulthood. The inner child is a metaphorical representation of your childhood self: the vulnerable, innocent, and curious part of you that experienced the world for the first time. When you experience emotional pain or trauma during your formative years, your inner child can become wounded and carry that pain with you into adulthood, where it can manifest as anxiety, depression, or avoidance. Inner child work helps you confront and heal these emotional wounds so that you can move forward with a greater sense of emotional freedom and clarity.

Inner child work is essential for those who want to heal their emotional wounds, develop a stronger sense of self-awareness, and step into empowerment. When you're able to connect with and heal your inner child, you can break free from patterns of behavior that are no longer serving you. You can cultivate more self-love, self-acceptance, and self-compassion, which ultimately paves the pathway to a life you can thrive in, instead of one where you are just surviving.

When you're feeling your feelings, the purpose of inner child work is to meet yourself in the pain and offer yourself the love that you didn't receive as a child. In Jackie's case, her inner child was carrying an immense amount of anger and sadness from the years she spent giving love to her parents but not receiving any in return. Even though she was in her mid-forties, the pain and sadness Jackie tried so desperately to avoid was actually the pain of her inner child, who had first experienced those emotions decades ago.

THE BASICS OF INNER CHILD WORK

Inner child work is best done somewhere safe and comfortable, ideally in the comfort of your own home, where you have access to comfy blankets, tissues, and lots of water. In fact, sometimes the most powerful inner child work happens when you're simply sitting on your couch, feeling your emotions and allowing yourself to explore the memories and experiences that come up.

Inner child work typically presents itself when you're in the acknowledgment phase of the "Feel Your Feelings" framework. The intention is to let that inner child's voice be safely expressed. Then, let the current version of yourself offer consolation, love, and support to the inner child. Let's use Jackie's story to illustrate the process.

1. **Acknowledge the emotion, sit with it, and practice non-judgment.** Recognize the emotion you're trying to avoid, and intentionally allow it in.

   • Jackie felt anger and sadness. She also noticed that she was feeling a touch of shame for carrying these emotions at all.

2. **Locate the inner child.** Ask yourself, *When was the first time I experienced this emotion?* You don't have to know the exact date or remember all the details of the initial pain; the most important thing is to identify the general time frame when the wounding began.

   • In Jackie's case, she couldn't recall one specific instance when these emotions were triggered because they were a pattern for most of her childhood. But she *could* remember the general age at which she started feeling the anger and sadness—about seven years old.

3. **Connect with the inner child.** Connect with the energy and the emotion that your inner child was (and is) feeling. This may feel intense or challenging at first as the emotions of the past start rushing back in. Stay with the feelings and breathe. It can also be helpful to find a picture of yourself from the time frame when the wounding began. Spend a few moments looking at a photo of younger you, and connect with the emotions that child was feeling.

   • Jackie dug up a photo from her first day of second grade. She was smiling in the photo, but Jackie remembers how much pain that little girl was actually feeling. She allowed those feelings to come up.

4. **Validate, validate, validate.** The first thing most of us want to do when we feel uncomfortable is fix the feeling. This is not the time to fix—it's time to validate. Place a hand on your heart, close your eyes, and begin to offer emotional validation for whatever your inner child is feeling. Emotional validation can sound like:

   • "I am so, so sorry that you feel unloved. I love you so, so much."

   • "I see how much pain you're in, and I want you to know that it's safe to feel that pain."

   • "You're right, it isn't fair that you were treated like that."

   • "You're allowed to feel sad and angry."

   • "I see you. I'm here for you. I'm holding you. I've got you."

   • "It's okay to feel this way."

   • "I see how much this is affecting you, and I want you to know how much I love you."

5. **Offer yourself the responses you needed to receive in childhood.** This step may naturally unfold as a part of your emotional validation, but if you hold any core memories that are still affecting you in present time, offer yourself the responses you wish you had received when the wounding first occurred.

   • All Jackie wanted was for her parents to spend time with her and offer her some of the emotional support she always had to give them. She began offering her inner child loving responses like "Little Jackie, your feelings are just as important as everybody else's. And they're important because *you're* important. You don't have to prove that to anyone. You *are* important, and I want to make sure you know that. I'm going to stay here with you, and I'm not going to leave you."

6. **Let the feelings flow.** If your inner child wants to have a tantrum, let them have the tantrum. If your inner child wants to just be sad, let the tears flow. Let the emotions come up. Stay present with them. Breathe into them. Let them out.

MORE INNER CHILD WORK

The practice of validating and nurturing the inner child is powerful in itself, but there are a number of other ways you can support your inner child and deepen your inner child work.

   • **Connect with your inner child through play.** Take some time to do something that you loved doing as a child. Play a game, buy yourself those fuzzy pink slippers you really wanted at the time, or engage in a creative activity that reminds you of your inner child, such as drawing, coloring, or crafting. Let your imagination flow freely. The purpose is to give your inner child permission to be a kid again, to celebrate that younger version of you and reconnect with the joy they deserved to feel.

- **Visualize your inner child.** Sit in a quiet place and close your eyes. Visualize yourself as a child. Then, imagine that you're sitting across from your child self, and you're holding both of their hands. What do they want to say to you? What do you want to say to them? Let the dialogue (and the accompanying emotions) evolve naturally. When you're finished, thank your inner child for coming on this journey with you.

- **Write a letter to your inner child.** Sit down with a pen and paper and write a letter to your inner child. Tell them that you love them, that you see them, and that you're there for them. Share with them any words of encouragement or support that you feel they need to hear. When you're finished, read the letter out loud to yourself. Let yourself feel the love you hold for that younger version of you. Let yourself feel that love for the current version of yourself too.

Journaling Prompts for Inner Child Work

Journaling can be a powerful tool for connecting with your inner child and exploring your past experiences and emotions. Here are some prompts to get you started.

- What are some of your earliest memories from childhood? Write about any specific moments, people, or places that stand out to you.

- Describe your inner child. How old do they feel? What do they look like? What emotions do they express?

- What were some of your favorite activities or hobbies as a child? How did they make you feel?
- Reflect on any negative experiences or challenges you faced as a child. How do those experiences still impact you today?
- Imagine having a conversation with your younger self. What advice or encouragement would you offer them?
- Think about your relationship with your caregivers or parents. How did they make you feel loved and supported?
- If you experienced emotional disconnection with your caregivers at any point, reflect on the experience that sticks out the most.
- Explore any unmet needs or desires you had as a child. How can you address or fulfill those needs now, as an adult?
- What were your dreams and aspirations as a child? Have any of them remained consistent throughout your life?
- What would you say if you wrote a letter of love and compassion to your inner child? Take this time to tell them that you are there for them and that they are worthy of love and happiness.

Remember, journaling is a personal and introspective process, so feel free to modify these prompts or create your own based on what resonates with you most. The goal is to create a safe space for exploring and healing your inner child. It can be helpful to work with a therapist or coach who has experience in this area. This work takes time and patience, and while it can be intense, it is a powerful and transformative way to address emotional avoidance. Remember, engaging in emotional avoidance is a natural response to difficult emotions, but it prevents you from fully experiencing and processing those emotions. By taking these steps to own your avoidance, you'll learn to listen to your emotions and use them as a guide for growth and healing.

Chapter Reflections

These journaling prompts are some of the very same questions I had Saul reflect on to get to the root of his own emotional avoidance. Though your personal narrative may differ from Saul's, the value of exploring your unique brand of avoidance remains.

- Do you avoid certain emotions within yourself? How do you do that?
- Do you avoid receiving emotional support or having emotional exchanges with others? Why?
- How might your emotional avoidance be sabotaging or delaying your healing?
- What is one action step you can take to begin addressing this avoidance? (For example, speaking to a counselor, journaling, or choosing to be present with the emotions themselves.)
- How does your behavioral avoidance show up? Do you throw yourself into work? Do you throw yourself into other people?
- What tangible tools do you use to avoid, and what do they do for you?
- Do substances like drugs or alcohol play into your behavioral avoidance?[20]

---

20. If you are struggling with substance abuse, please refer to the back of this book for resources and support.

- How might your behavioral avoidance be sabotaging or delaying your healing? How much time do your avoidance behaviors take up?
- What healthy habits, activities, or practices can you choose to engage in instead of your unhealthy avoidance behaviors?

Chapter Summary

Healing requires taking ownership of your avoidance and allowing yourself to fully feel your feelings. By acknowledging and accepting your emotions and cultivating healthy emotional processing, you will develop a deeper relationship with yourself. Two key ways to engage in this healing are inner child work and examining your early-stage emotional development.

Chapter Seven
EXPLORE YOUR TRIGGERS

Now that you're connected to your soul guidance and are learning to taking up more space, it's time for some of the nitty-gritty anxiety transformation work: exploring and understanding your triggers. My use of the word *trigger* refers to any person, place, thing, thought, idea, or memory that activates your anxiety. You may already know what most of your triggers are, but work is about more than just knowing. In this chapter, we're going to explore how your triggers feel, what negative beliefs they perpetuate, and how they influence your reactions. Once you've gathered that information, you'll be well-equipped to respond to your triggers in new ways rather than react to them or avoid them altogether.

As nice as it would be to exist in a trigger-free utopia, it's just not possible. Trust me, I've tried; I had a long phase of fantasizing about running away to a cabin in the woods where I could escape technology, social interactions, and judgment from others. The fantasy sounded so good, in fact, that I actually started looking into it, even though I knew deep down that isolation wasn't the solution. Sure, I could leave a few of my big triggers behind, but I'd still be left with a big, ticking time bomb of anxiety: myself.

You can't run away from what activates you. The goal here isn't to never be activated or anxious again—the goal is to better understand yourself so that you can better support yourself. The more you understand your anxiety, the better equipped you'll be to introduce new ways of responding. In my opinion, some of the best opportunities for healing and growth lie within your triggers.

A Deep-Dive into What Activates You

The following exercise offers a framework to help you explore and understand your triggers. You'll start by listing out your triggers and then will log a few additional reflections for each one. I'll walk you through it step-by-step, but a quick disclaimer before we dive in: I recommend working through this exercise on a computer. This is a rare exception, as I usually recommend writing by hand during self-reflection work. But, for better or worse, I'm still a child of the technology age. I love a good spreadsheet now and again to organize my thoughts. If you don't have access to a computer (or you'd prefer do the following exercise by hand) that's absolutely fine; you can draw or create columns in your journal instead.

EXERCISE
Trigger Identification Sheet

To get started, create five columns, and label each of the columns as follows: Trigger, Body Location, Negative Belief, Reaction, and Response. It should look something like this.

Trigger	Body Location	Negative Belief	Reaction	Response

1. Fill out column one, labeled "Trigger." This column is
   pretty self-explanatory: fill it with whatever you believe
   triggers your anxiety. If trying to remember and write
   down *all* of your triggers feels overwhelming, call back
   to your soul dialogue work to help you organize your
   thoughts. For example, if your biggest soul work is about
   body acceptance, focus on the specific things that trigger
   anxiety about your body image.

   You can write down triggers in real time, starting today.
   Or, you can approach this list as a "look back" on the past
   few months by documenting specific triggers that you
   can remember clearly. Personally, I like to take a blended
   approach: with my soul work in mind, I'll reflect on the
   past month or so, and then I will continue to come back
   to my log when a new, relevant trigger occurs.

2. When you're ready, fill out column two, labeled "Body
   Location." When you experience that trigger, where do you
   feel it in your body? What does it feel like? Knowing how
   you feel in your body is a powerful tool for navigating your
   anxiety, and it's likely you'll find that your body responds
   to some triggers differently than others. Maybe you experience chest tightness when you're overwhelmed, but you
   feel a drop in your stomach when you're lonely. If you're
   having a day where *everything* seems to be activating you,
   and you can't keep up with your mind, look to your body.
   What are you feeling? What does that feeling usually mean
   for you? Knowing where you feel things can help you figure out what tools or practices you need most.

3. Then, fill out column three, labeled "Negative Belief." What negative belief about yourself did that trigger fuel or "confirm"? Even if you know the negative belief about yourself isn't true (spoiler alert: none of them are), allow yourself to be honest about what the anxious or wounded part of you feels. It can be a scary act of vulnerability to write down your core negative beliefs, so please kind to yourself if shame or judgment try to creep in while you're working. If anything, I encourage you to drum up a little excitement here. Why? Because you're calling out your negative beliefs. You're seeing them as separate from you. Eventually, you'll remember that they were never a part of you at all.

4. Finally, fill out column four, labeled "Reaction." Write out how you reacted when you're triggered. Also include how you felt the rest of the day, the quality of your inner dialogue, and any other notes about your reactions. Get as specific as possible here—your reactions are the patterns that must be broken. Keep in mind that sometimes your reaction might look a lot like inaction. When my anxiety would get super activated, I'd typically shut down. From an outsider's point of view, it might not have seemed like I was anxious or triggered at all. Be sure to search yourself for these kinds of silent reactions too.

Here is an example of what one row of a trigger chart may look like. (Leave column five blank for now—we will come back to it later.)

Trigger	Body Location	Negative Belief	Reaction	Response
I hadn't looked at my phone all day, and when I finally *did* look hours later, nobody had texted me.	I felt an anxious pit in my stomach, accompanied by feelings of sadness all over.	Nobody in my life cares about me.	I didn't tell anyone how I felt. Also felt extra anxious/upset when I saw some friends later that week.	

This exercise does not need to be completed all in one sitting. I suggest taking at least a few days to fill out your reflections, especially if this is your first time exploring your anxiety triggers. It's normal for some funky emotions to come up too, so please take breaks if you start feeling overwhelmed. Compassion is the name of the game.

You won't need to work with this template forever; it's simply a way to help you to build some emotional muscle memory. I've worked with clients who used this format religiously for months, while others only needed it for a few days. Some clients use this template intermittently. (Once in a while, I'll even come back to this practice myself!) Eventually, the structure of this template will become an automated inner process: you'll learn to recognize in both body and mind when you're activated, you'll recognize the core belief, and you'll find the space within yourself to choose a new response over your patterned reactions. This exercise is the scaffolding of your transformation. It's chock-full of information that can be used to fuel your journey from anxiety to empowerment.

Let's unpack a few of ways you can glean insights from your trigger identification work. You now have a bird's-eye view of your anxiety, your triggers, and your reactions. If you were able to fill out all of the columns for each trigger, you've now got a Mad Libs–style script to help you articulate the patterns you want to change: "When [trigger] happens, it makes me feel [body location] and fuels the story of [negative belief]."

Even if you don't share what you're feeling with anyone else, it's important to be able to clearly articulate what's going on to yourself. Doing so allows you to acknowledge and take ownership of your emotions—and it's much harder to avoid your truths when you've written them down.

By completing this exercise, you've also created another self-awareness touchpoint that will spark more ideas about how to better care for yourself. For example, if you noticed that certain people in your life all seem to trigger the same negative self-belief in you, perhaps it's time to examine those relationships. If a lot of your triggers happen when you're sleep-deprived, how can you begin to prioritize rest? If you've realized that you store most of your anxiety in your upper body, how can you start to release some of that tension? See where I'm going here? Use your responses as a tool to deepen the ways in which you care for yourself.

Turn Your Reactions into Responses

Perhaps my favorite part of trigger identification work is how the reactions you observed (in column four of your worksheet) can be expanded upon to fuel your growth. I'd like you to read through the reactions you wrote down, then reflect on the following questions.

- **Is there a larger theme or pattern in your reactions?** Are your reactions more internal (shutting down, getting quiet, etc.) or external (talking louder or more, getting angry, etc.)?
- **Where did you learn your reactions?** For example, if your automatic reaction is to get angry or yell, was that a reaction learned in childhood?
- **Do your reactions feel like a choice, or do they feel automatic?** Historically, have you been able to find a pause to think about your reactions, or do you react first and think later? Explain.

If you feel like most—or all—of your reactions are automatic, you're not alone. It may have felt like you weren't choosing your reactions consciously, as you were repeating a familiar reaction that's been reinforced over time. In many cases, reactivity is learned in childhood. Your reactivity may either be a response to your caregivers growing up (they yelled, so you stayed quiet) or a carbon copy of their reactivity (they would shut down emotionally, so you do the same). Understanding where your reactive patterns come from is a part of the healing process and can help to soften any self-blame or judgment you hold about your reactions. They were simply learned behaviors, and you're now in the process of unlearning them. Transformation lies in your ability to disrupt those automatic reactions and practice new, empowered responses instead. In other words, you've got to train yourself to respond to your triggers instead of reacting to them.

The first step in practicing responsiveness is deciding how you'd like to respond instead. Do this ahead of time. Trust me, it's a whole lot easier to practice a new, healthier response to a trigger when you have plan in place. Once you have clearly identified how you want to respond, you'll feel more comfortable and confident in your ability to do so. When the trigger arises in real life, you'll be better prepared to respond in a way that aligns with your highest and best good. Practicing responsiveness is a process, and it will take time and effort to build new habits and patterns of behavior. Naturally, having a plan doesn't guarantee you'll execute responsiveness perfectly, but perfection isn't the goal! The true goal is to develop and practice healthier ways of coping when you're triggered.

Another important piece of learning to respond instead of react is your ability to slow down and ground yourself before you react. Use the tools you now have (like The Five Senses exercise from chapter 1, or Sensation-Shifting Breathing from chapter 2) to call yourself back into your body before you react. Learning to slow down when you're triggered is a big practice in patience. Aside from the fact that the anxiety brain just isn't used to going slow, we've also been culturally conditioned to expect things to happen fast. We're living in the age of instant gratification! If you want to order a hamburger, it can be at your door in twenty minutes. If you want to order some new shoes, you'll get them within a few days. If you want to talk to a friend, you can say hello almost instantaneously with a quick tap-tap-tap on your phone. Long-term emotional change (like developing strategies for responsiveness) just doesn't happen at the same speed. You've got to learn to play the long game here. Be gentle with yourself and your expectations.

Develop Your Responses

You'll want to pull up your trigger identification sheet again. It's time to fill out column five, titled "Responses."

Brainstorming new responses is fairly self-explanatory: for each of the reactions documented on your trigger ID sheet, write down your ideal response. I want you to challenge yourself a little bit, but make sure your responses are both accessible *and* safe. For example, if one of your triggers is a person with whom you've had trauma, I advise against a goal like "My response is to learn how to not be triggered by them at all," which isn't a fair expectation and may invalidate your own healing. A safe, more accessible response might be something like "When I'm triggered by this person, I will practice calmly removing myself from the situation." If you're not sure how to replace your reactions with safe, accessible responses, consider reaching out to a trauma-informed professional who can provide you with additional support.

There's one other thing I want you to keep in mind while you're brainstorming: allow your soul guidance to inform your responses. Connect this nitty-gritty work back to the bigger picture of your transformation by ensuring your responses feel both healing and empowering.

As an example, here is a story about my client Colette, who allowed her soul guidance to deepen her response strategy.

Colette often found herself triggered when her partner took "too long" to respond to a question she had asked via text. The feeling in her body was both tight and heavy at once. She felt a pit in her stomach and tightness across her chest. Her usual reaction to a trigger like this is to personalize ("I'm annoying them and they don't want to talk to me") and catastrophize ("They are going to break up with me"). These anxious thoughts would build in her mind and typically caused her to fire off a string of angry, hurt texts.

Colette knew that her preferred initial response would be to take a few deep breaths, practice Truth versus Story, and hold off on sending texts riddled with negative assumptions. In Colette's soul work, which she had been reflecting on prior to this trigger, she recognized that she was being called to work on her overall self-worth.

So, Colette paired that soul guidance with her initial response strategy to practice an upleved, soul-guided response.

This meant that the next time Colette was triggered, in addition to taking a pause and practicing Truth versus Story, she also practiced shifting her thoughts to ones that were more compassionate and self-loving. Once Colette was able to ground herself through her breath, she thought back to scenarios when she felt loving and connected to herself. As she reflected on those moments, she started to bring some of those feelings back in to her body. She even began to integrate mantras like "I love myself. I am worthy of love." In this way, Colette restrained herself from reacting to the anxiety she felt.

In this example, Colette's initial response was already fantastic, and her soul-guided response only amplified the practice. Note how Colette's response strategy was specific. Rather than deciding she would like to "respond more calmly" when she was triggered, she made a plan for *how* she would respond calmly: she'd breathe, tend to her thoughts, and practice restraint in messaging her partner until she had more information.

When you're coming up with your own responses, watch out for vague suggestions like "I would like to respond better" or "I'd like to find a way to deal with my emotions." *How* would you do that? Be specific. There's no such thing as a perfect plan, but coming up with some suggestions ahead of time is valuable.

Plus, it's your response strategy to practice! If a response doesn't feel right or isn't helpful, you have full permission to try again in a new way. This doesn't have to be a heavy work. Let it be empowering. (And, I daresay, let it be fun!) You have the information you need to start coming up with supportive, healthy responses, and now it's time for you to take this material into your own hands. If you've filled out column five in your trigger identification sheet, you should now have a handy-dandy list of responses to practice!

Two common fears come up whenever I teach this work to my students. They worry that it'll be too hard, and they're afraid they're going to fail. If you're having similar thoughts, allow me to share some tough love with you: it may be hard, and you probably will fail at least a few times. But remember, "hard" doesn't mean "bad," failing doesn't mean you suck, and neither of those two fears is justification for giving up on yourself.

Change is difficult, and sitting in the uncomfortable space between "safe" responses and new behaviors isn't exactly a walk in the park either. I promise you, though, you can do it. After all, you're more prepared now than you've ever been. You're aware of your anxiety triggers, you understand your patterns, and you're committed to (or at least curious about) implementing new, empowered responses to replace your automatic reactions. That's all you need to start practicing.

Chapter Reflections

Pull out the responses you wrote in the previous section. Then, use the following questions to reflect on how you'll keep yourself accountable, motivated, and connected to utilizing your new, empowered responses.

- Reflect on your current methods of holding yourself accountable to implement these empowered responses. Are there any specific strategies or support systems you can put in place to ensure you stay on track?
- Consider the areas in your life where you might face the most challenges in employing these new responses. How can you proactively address these challenges and maintain your commitment to positive change?

- How will you remind yourself of the importance of these empowered responses during moments of stress or triggering events? Are there any visual cues, affirmations, or grounding techniques you can incorporate into your daily routine to reinforce your commitment?
- Think about the benefits of responding to triggers with mindfulness and empowerment. How do you believe these new responses will positively impact your relationships, emotional well-being, and overall quality of life?
- Visualize yourself navigating triggering situations with grace and empowered responses. How does it feel to act from a place of self-awareness and mindfulness? What positive outcomes do you envision as a result of these new responses?

Chapter Summary

Observing your personal anxiety triggers and automatic responses will help you cultivate self-awareness and gain insight into your patterns of reactivity. With this awareness, you can consciously choose to respond in more mindful and empowered ways that align with your true self.

Implementation Break

Congratulations on completing part 2 of this book. Now, it's time to pause and take a well-deserved implementation break. During this break, allow yourself to integrate the knowledge and practices you've encountered. Take some time for self-care, engage in activities that bring you joy, and savor the sense of accomplishment that comes with self-discovery.

PART THREE

EMBODIMENT
AND
EMPOWERMENT

Chapter Eight
RETRAIN YOUR MIND

Welcome back! I hope your integration break was supportive for you. And boy, am I excited for us to jump into part 3 of this book!

By this point, you should be feeling much more aware of your emotions, your patterns, and your responses. You have a toolkit that's been filled with exercises and frameworks to support your healing, and now, we're ready to talk empowerment.

It's time to start thinking and feeling from a more empowered state of mind, which involves learning to replace negative or anxious thoughts with positive ones. As I shared earlier in this book, starting your anxiety transformation journey with thought-replacement work isn't effective. If your body doesn't feel safe, or if you aren't aware of your emotions and patterns, the anxious mind isn't going to be able to accept new, empowered thoughts—there's just no space for them. This is why we addressed the mind-body connection in part 1 and did so much emotional healing in part 2: you've been getting your inner world ready to practice thought replacement effectively! In this chapter, you will begin to teach your mind to think better, more empowered thoughts. Thoughts that…

- Are grounded in truth.
- Will stop a negative or anxious spiral.
- Emphasize possibility and how much you're capable of, and
- Elicit positive feelings about yourself.

Retraining Your Mind through Empowered Replacement Thoughts

The method for retraining your mind is straightforward: take each anxious thought and replace it with a positive thought. Traditional psychology refers to this work as "negative thought replacement." The self-help community calls it "the power of positive thinking." In Vedic tradition, it's mantra work. Regardless of what discipline or language we use, the work is the same: you are training your mind and body to think differently. But this work is not as simple as it sounds.

I had a client named Adam who was in the middle of some pretty serious money struggles. He had a few very large hospital bills, collections agencies were calling him nonstop, and he was working a dead-end job. Adam knew he had to change something, but he was so paralyzed by his anxiety that it was nearly impossible for him to think straight. Adam would call me and say things like, "Amanda, I just don't see a way out of this. I'm going to be broke forever. Why do I bother even trying?"

One day, I asked him, "Adam, do you really believe you'll be broke forever? Do you really think you'll never get out of this?"

He paused, took a few deep breaths, and said no. Adam had been doing his inner work long enough to recognize that his anxiety was causing him to react negatively. In that moment, he had already exercised his ability to calm his nervous system and reconnect to the truth, so I knew he was more than capable of practicing empowered thought replacement.

In order for Adam to take control of his anxiety, he had to become a watchdog of his own mind. Every time he wanted to go into a negative spiral, like he had when he called me, his job was to replace the negative thoughts about himself with ones that were empowering and focused on possibility. Something like, "I have the power to change my situation, and I'm going to choose to find a way out of this." What practicing a replacement thought like that did for him was offer a reminder that his experience was temporary. It allowed him to self-soothe and collect himself so that he could get out of the anxiety spin cycle and take empowered next steps to change his situation.

How to Find Your Empowered Replacement Thoughts

There are a number of ways to come up with empowered replacement thoughts for yourself. One of the easiest ways to construct better thoughts is to direct challenge the negative thought in your mind. Ask yourself if the thought is realistic, helpful, or evidence-based. Often, negative thoughts are based on assumptions or beliefs that aren't necessarily true. When I want to challenge a negative thought, I like to ask questions like:

- "Says who?"
- "Where did I get that idea from?"
- "Is this thought even mine to begin with?"

Then, flip the anxious thought into something better. Start by identifying the negative thought and ask yourself, *What's the opposite of what my brain is saying to me right now?* Then, craft a statement that embodies that opposite thought.

In Adam's case, his negative thought was *I'm going to be broke forever*. One could argue that the exact opposite thought would be something like *I'm a bajillionaire and I don't ever have to worry about money*, but that thought wasn't something that Adam could authentically connect with. An empowered thought like *I'm not going to be broke forever. I have the power to change my situation, and I'm going to choose to find a way out of this* was much more resonant. Not only did that statement feel more accessible and true for Adam, it empowered him to start taking action on his situation.

You can also create empowered thoughts by approaching the negative thoughts from a place of curiosity. When your negative inner dialogue is especially heavy, it can feel harder to find an empowered replacement thought. That's where a lighter, more curious energy can come in handy. By asking yourself questions like "What's the better story to tell in this moment?" or "What else could be true here?" you allow yourself to explore alternative perspectives that might feel more empowering.

For instance, let's say you're feeling anxious about an upcoming presentation at work. You might be telling yourself, *I'm going to screw this up and embarrass myself in front of everyone*. Instead of accepting that thought as the truth, you could approach it with curiosity and ask, "What's the better story to tell in this moment?" Perhaps you realize that you've given successful presentations before and have valuable insights to share. Or maybe you realize that even if things don't go perfectly, it's not the end of the world, and you'll still have the opportunity to learn and grow from the experience.

My all-time favorite way to find empowered thoughts is to ask the question, "What's the best-case scenario right now?" Anxious thoughts want to find the bad ending in all scenarios, so they dwell on everything that could go wrong; an empowered mind wants to explore the happy ending and instead dwells on all of the things that could go right. For example, if someone with dating anxiety really wanted a relationship and had thoughts like *I'm never going to find my person. I'm going to be alone forever*, I'm going to assume that thought probably isn't creating a best-case scenario mindset. Empowered thoughts like *I am an incredible person. Whoever my person is, they're going to be lucky as hell to be with me!* is a much better fit. It focuses on the best-case scenario instead of the worst, and it brings self-love back into focus.

You can also create empowered replacement thoughts by channeling your empowerment role model. This can be an author or leader you love, a friend, or another figure in your life that inspires you. This should be someone who embodies qualities that you admire and want to bring out more in yourself. Imagine yourself stepping into their shoes, and ask yourself, *What would my empowerment role model do in this situation?* Close your eyes and imagine yourself in their presence. Think about how they would approach the situation and what actions they would take. Use this as a guide to help you make decisions and take action in a way that aligns with your values and goals.

This visualization is a fun, simple way to break free from the anxious mind's perspective, and it can help you create thoughts from a more empowered viewpoint. Now, of course, you aren't meant to become a carbon copy of your role model. Use them as a source of motivation and guidance, but craft empowered responses in your unique voice and tone. Empowered replacement thoughts should always feel true to you and how you speak, and they should resonate with your situation. For example, if you're not the kind of person to say "I am a divine goddess" but you like the energy of that message, what would be *your* take on it? How would you say it? Find your interpretation, then use it. Your empowered replacement thoughts will stick better when they really sound like something you'd say.

Activating Your Authentic, Empowered Feelings

The secret to long-lasting empowered thoughts? Creating the empowered feelings that go along with them. The mind and body are intricately connected and are constantly communicating with each other. The body has its own way of processing and responding to information, and it often provides important feedback to the mind. When we try to replace negative thoughts with positive ones, it can sometimes feel like we are simply trying to convince ourselves of something that may not be entirely true.

When you can effectively elicit the positive feelings associated with your empowered thoughts, your body will start to trust those thoughts more. When those empowered thoughts are validated by the positive response in your body, your subconscious mind becomes more open to generating more empowered thoughts; it creates a ton of positive momentum. This is why it's so important to choose empowered thoughts that are accessible and have some level of believability. When you focus on creating empowered thoughts that feel true and authentic in your body, your brain is more likely to believe them and integrate them into your daily thinking. The body responds to the truth of a new thought, and when you experience it as true on a physical level, it reinforces the message to your mind.

The challenge, of course, is getting into that feeling state. I really struggled to understand this at first. A core part of my own anxiety was rooted in a belief that I was unworthy of love. When I was learning to integrate empowered replacements thoughts like *I am loved*, I'd get frustrated and think, *I can't make my body feel love when I just don't feel it.* How could my brain tell my body to feel something without having the proof of that thing?

You too might find it hard to "create" an empowered feeling like confidence or self-love using just your thoughts, but it's more possible than you realize. In fact, you're inherently capable of it. Your thoughts create physical responses in your body—without proof—all the time! Have you ever thought about your favorite meal and noticed your mouth was beginning to water? Have you ever had a "spicy" thought and started to physically become aroused? In either case, all you did was direct your thoughts to something you'd previously experienced, and your body responded.

Nostalgia is another great example of this. If I asked you to tell me, in great detail, about the happiest moment of your life, I bet you'd start to feel a little bit of that same joy you experienced as you described it to me. Where your thoughts and attention go, energy flows.

You don't actually need to have the "proof" of the emotion to create physical feelings in the body—you just have to bring up a memory of the desired emotion, then bring that feeling into your body. If you want to activate empowered thoughts and feelings regarding self-confidence, call forward a memory of the last time you felt that way. If you want to work on feelings of security and stability, choose a memory that reminds you of what that feels like. This is a little trick I like to call "firelog memories."

FIRELOG MEMORIES

First, let me explain where I got this name from. If you've ever gone camping or created a fire in your fireplace, you'll know that it's easier to buy one of those store-bought, scientifically engineered firelogs. They ignite easily, and as the fire from this special log grows, it eventually spreads to the rest of the logs. The firelog, in this context, is not the sole log fueling the fire—it simply serves as the catalyst for the flames to grow. In other words, that firelog isn't the only piece of wood in the fire, but it is a very powerful one.

Your firelog memories are thoughts and experiences that can catalyze an empowered feeling. When I was working on empowered thoughts like *I am loved*, I would meditate on specific memories with my family that started to generate positive feelings of love in my body. I'd do my best to mark how that felt in my body, and I practiced keeping my body in that feeling state for as long as I could after the meditation ended. The more I practiced this, the easier it became for me to activate positive, empowered feelings through my thoughts alone.

Now, let's say you're working on activating feelings of self-confidence, but you don't think you have any firelog memories that would fully activate feelings of confidence. Even if you don't have an obvious memory to use, I bet you've had a taste of what confidence feels like before. Maybe you felt confident while singing along to your favorite song, or you felt the confidence of the protagonist in your favorite book. Those experiences, however small or insignificant they may seem to you, still count!

By activating positive emotions associated with empowering experiences, you will reinforce the belief systems that are worth keeping. If you encounter resistance to these beliefs, use your firelog memories to reactivate the positive feelings and move through the body's resistance. Additionally, you can practice this technique through meditation using the following script.

EXERCISE
Firelog Memories Meditation

Begin by finding a comfortable seated position, either in a chair or on the floor. Allow your hands to rest comfortably in your lap, and gently close your eyes.

1. Take a deep breath in through your nose, filling your lungs with air, and then slowly exhale through your mouth.

2. Focus your attention on your breath, observing the sensation of the air moving in and out of your body. As you inhale, imagine a bright light filling your body with energy.

3. As you exhale, see that light clear away any thoughts of disempowerment or anxiety.

4. Choose one of your firelog memories and begin to see yourself in that experience again. Allow the memory to be as real and vivid as possible. What were you wearing? What was the weather like? What did your environment sound, look, and smell like? Create all of the different tones of reality, and let yourself rest there for a moment.

5. Then, focus on yourself within that memory. If it was a time when you felt super confident, for example, put yourself back at that exact moment. Why did you feel confident? How did that feel? What was happening around you?

6. Recreate the full scenario, and allow yourself to experience it in your mind's eye as if it were happening right now.

7. Give yourself a few minutes to bask in the positive feelings you activated in your body. Pay attention to how this felt. Did you feel a sense of spaciousness across your chest? Did you feel energized? Lighter? These observations can provide you with more information that will help you activate the positive feelings.

8. When you're ready, take a deep breath in, then slowly exhale. Gently wiggle your fingers and toes and slowly open your eyes.

After completing your meditation, practice keeping those positive feelings in your body for as long as you can. When you're practicing thought replacement, bring these feelings and emotions back into the body as you think or say the new, empowered thoughts.

Sticky Notes

Sticky notes with positive affirmations are another simple way to activate your empowered thought and feelings. To create a tangible reminder of your empowered thoughts, start by identifying a few areas in your life where you would like to change negative thought patterns. Write down corresponding affirmations that support those areas on colorful sticky notes. Place the notes in visible locations, such as your kitchen cabinets, your computer screen, or your fridge. Choose locations that you walk by frequently so that the affirmations catch your attention multiple times throughout the day. Seeing your empowered thoughts regularly will help impress them onto your subconscious mind, and reciting them aloud will help you practice activating the empowered feelings.

One of my clients, Diana, particularly loved this exercise. Diana was working on her anxiety around boundary-setting with a demanding boss, and she'd feel the most anxious while getting ready for work in the mornings. She wrote out little notes that affirmed her ability to stand up for herself, things like "I have a voice that deserves to be heard," "'No' is a complete sentence," and "I feel empowered when I set boundaries." She stuck those colorful sticky notes in all of her "getting ready" places: her bathroom mirror, her closet door, and above her kitchen sink. When she would pass by one of those spaces, the colorful notes would catch her eye, and the empowering reminders helped her interrupt her anxious thoughts.

Diana repeated the affirmations aloud, and over time, she noticed the way she was repeating the mantras was changing. She was no longer quietly repeating empowered thoughts to herself—she was courageously claiming them as her truth. Diana's growing sense of self-empowerment was become more clear in her tone, in her mind, and in her body, and that felt sense of empowerment catalyzed her transformation.

Even though Diana's workplace anxiety is a thing of the past now, she still uses her sticky note affirmations as a way to ground herself each morning.

The Power of Lived Gratitude

Gratitude is the rocket fuel of your self-empowerment journey. When you regularly focus on what you're grateful for, you're essentially training your brain to look for the good in life. The ability to shift your focus away from what's lacking in your life and on to what's going well builds the same mental muscle that you use when shifting your thoughts from anxious to empowered.

The potency of your gratitude practices lies in your ability to actually feel grateful. Personally, gratitude lists never really did much for me. Whenever I'd sit down to make a list of things I was grateful for in my journal, I found myself listing out the same few things over and over again. It felt more like a task than a supportive tool. Instead, I focus my energy on lived gratitude: finding (and feeling) the good in the moment, as those moments happened.

A lived gratitude practice requires nothing more than your commitment to pausing when you notice something that makes you happy in some way. And when you turn your attention to those little moments, actually let yourself be in them. Savor these happy moments, no matter how small they seem. For example, the next time you walk outside on a beautiful sunny day, slow down. Close your eyes for a second or two and feel the warmth of the sun on your skin. If you have a thought like *Mmm, this is nice*, be in the literal appreciation of that thought. Let that one happy thought appreciate, or grow, into another positive thought. Lived gratitude is an active practice of expression; it's about how deeply you allow yourself to feel into a positive moment.

The more positive moments you allow yourself to feel, the more positive you will begin to feel overall. Lived gratitude is a powerful practice for the small moments, but don't forget about the big ones, too—like your current personal journey from anxiety to empowerment. Practicing lived, felt gratitude for the progress you've made so far will help cultivate long-term self-love and will serve as motivation as you continued to make more self-empowered decisions in mind, body, and soul.

Additionally, practicing lived gratitude for your journey with anxiety will help you feel more connected to yourself, others, and the world around you. When you take the time to appreciate the people, experiences, and things in your life, you may feel a sense of joy and fulfillment. It will also help you reframe challenges and setbacks as opportunities for growth and learning instead of as failures.

EXERCISE
Twenty-Four Hours of Lived Gratitude

Of course, I want you to integrate lived gratitude into your life consistently, but there's something extra special about consciously setting aside a day where your sole focus is on expressing sincere feelings of appreciation for the things that show up in your life. Why not kick-start your appreciation practice with a dedicated day?

Your Lived Gratitude Day begins tomorrow, no matter when you're reading this. As part of your morning routine, you'll set the intention to notice and appreciate as many moments as possible throughout the day. I want you do this tomorrow so that you won't be able to put it off or overthink it. Even if your day is already hectic or you have something unpleasant on your calendar, Lived Gratitude Day is still tomorrow. In fact, having Lived Gratitude Day fall on a difficult day can help diffuse any overwhelm or intensity.

At the following points throughout your day tomorrow, find a pause and drop into feelings of appreciation for that moment:

- When you wake up
- On your commute to work
- During your bathroom breaks
- During time spent outside

- After interacting with other people
- When you get back to your home, or finish work for the day
- While in the shower
- When your head hits the pillow before bed

See where this practice takes you! Embracing the challenge of Lived Gratitude Day is an opportunity to shift your perspective and cultivate gratitude, even amidst difficult circumstances.

Chapter Reflections

- What empowered thoughts are you working on, and why? Explain the nature of these empowered thoughts. For example, "I'm working on changing my self-deprecating thoughts into more empowered thoughts of self-love. This is because…"

- What positive feelings are associated with those empowered thoughts? If you're working on empowered thoughts about self-love, what does self-love feel like in your body? What does love feel like in your body? Describe this in as much detail as you can.

- What memories or experiences can you use to activate those positive feelings? Describe in detail the experiences you've had in the past that you can use to active positive feelings.

  - If you're having a hard time finding memories that would activate the exact positive feeling, find a memory that is similar enough. For example, I had a hard time finding memories that would activate feelings self-love in my body, but as a pet owner, I did know what unconditional love felt like. I used to practice bringing up feelings of how much I loved my dog and paid attention to how those feelings of love felt.

Chapter Summary

Empowered thought replacement is a valuable tool that allows you to swap negative thoughts for more positive ones. When you activate empowered feelings along with those new thoughts, your mind and body will better integrate this new belief system. With continued practice and self-awareness, you have the power to transform your mindset, overcome challenges, and create a life that is aligned with your empowered self.

Chapter Nine
THE IMPORTANCE OF COMPASSION

Now is a good time to remind you that your journey from anxiety to empowerment requires heaping doses of compassion. You're teaching yourself to work with the anxious mind in a new way, you're exploring emotional healing, and you're learning to make more mindful, soul-guided responses—that's a lot of (incredible) work! It's also work that takes time and patience.

Inner work isn't a guarantee that you'll never feel anxious again; it's an insurance plan for when you do. There will inevitably be moments where you feel stuck, or perhaps even frustrated that your anxiety hasn't magically gone away yet. However, what you're building right now is your emotional response system to existing triggers so that, no matter what comes up in the future, you've got tools to use. As you continue to practice new emotional responses over time, the intensity and duration of your anxiety will lessen. What once felt like a giant, earth-shattering trigger might reduce itself to just a tiny little nudge, a nudge you feel capable of addressing.

What if that is the key to feeling empowered? Knowing that you have the tools, that you trust yourself, and that you know what to do when things feel overwhelming. The dictionary definition of empowerment is: "power to influence or command thought, opinion, or behavior."[21] You have always had that power. It's just that now, you're learning to exercise that power in a different, bigger way. Empowerment has nothing to do with perfection and isn't defined by achieving a goal. Empowerment is about the act of choosing yourself, over and over again. My hope is that now, having exercised your power through some pretty deep reflections and inner work, you're able to see and appreciate your inherent power more clearly.

If you still feel like you have too much work to do to be fully empowered, listen up: I want you to toss that all-or-nothing mentality into the garbage. You can be proud of your growth *and* still want to grow more. You can appreciate where you are *and* have your sights sets on where you're going. This is where your ability to be compassionate toward yourself becomes essential. When you show yourself kindness and understanding, even when you stumble or make mistakes, you're offering yourself the support and encouragement your soul needs to keep moving forward. Self-compassion also helps you cultivate a positive and nurturing inner voice, which can counteract the negative self-talk that often accompanies anxiety. When you treat yourself with compassion, you are more likely to be patient, gentle, and understanding with yourself, which creates a safe and supportive environment for you to embody your empowerment.

---

21. *Merriam-Webster*, s.v. "authority (*n*.)," accessed October 27, 2023, https://www.merriam-webster.com/dictionary/authority.

Reframing Mess Ups with Compassion

You've got to make some room for mess ups. I know it can be frustrating when you know how you want to show up but your body or your mind (or both) don't want to get on board just yet. You're allowed to feel that frustration, and I encourage you to do so! Cry, vent about it in your journal, or go for a run. Do your best to keep that frustration from turning into self-shame or judgment.

Anxious folks tend to be perfectionists. We want to do things right, we want to have reached our goals already, and we want to have control. When that's not possible, we fault ourselves and all compassion goes out the window. Without self-compassion, you'll quickly fall into negative self-talk and self-blame, which only fuels anxiety and delays your transformation. It's important to recognize that perfectionism is often rooted in fear: fear of failure, fear of judgment, or fear of not being enough. When you learn to reframe your "mess ups" with compassion and approach your process with kindness and understanding, you break the cycle of perfectionism. Acknowledge that you're human, and slow progress, making mistakes, or even feeling like you've gone backward at times are all natural parts of the learning process.

Journal Prompts for Compassionate Reframing

When you feel yourself getting frustrated with your growth, rather than faulting or judging yourself for where you're at, practice compassionately reframing your experience. Here are a few journal prompts that can help with that process.

- **How can you be okay with where you are right now?** Take a deep breath and come back to truth. What do your mind, body, and soul need from you in order to be okay with where you are and how you're feeling?

- **Do you feel pressure to be somewhere (or someone) else right now? Where is that pressure coming from?** Is the pressure coming from you? How about your ego? What about your friends, your environment, or societal expectations? Look for what makes you feel like "should" have it all figured out by now.

  - **What can you do to release that pressure?** For example, if someone else is pressuring you to heal or grow on their timeline, ask yourself if you need to set a boundary with that person. If the pressure is self-created, you might opt to practice some mantra work or a forgiveness meditation.

- **Is this moment trying to teach you something? Is there more for you to learn here?** The truth is, you are *exactly* where you need to be, and there are lessons to be found in stuckness and frustration. You can further this reflection with questions like:

  - What purpose is this moment serving? Is it to teach you compassion, letting go, balance, or something else?

  - What are you not seeing about this circumstance right now?

- **What can you be proud of right now?** The best antidote for self-judgment is self-celebration. Find the things that are going well. Find the things you're proud of yourself for.

- **How can you be more gentle with yourself?** Look for ways you can soften the harshness of your self-judgment. How can you give yourself a break or offer yourself more love?

Keep an eye out for how much you're "should"-ing too. "Should" statements often come from societal or internalized expectations, and they are a surefire way to delay your healing. Statements like "I should know better" or "I shouldn't feel so overwhelmed right now" are a form of emotional invalidation and self-shame. Instead, notice when your "should"s come up, and try to meet them with more emotionally affirming inner dialogue. Here are a few of my favorite emotional validation mantras that come in super handy when challenging my "should"s.

- My pace is perfect.
- I'm exactly where I need to be right now.
- It's okay to feel what I'm feeling.
- My emotions aren't a sign of weakness; they're a sign of my humanity.
- My growth isn't a race, it's a journey.
- I trust the timing of my life.

It's Not a Regression, It's a Lesson

I don't believe in the concept of regression for those on a healing journey. Healing is not a linear process! Setbacks and challenges are a normal part of growth, and they do not mean you've gone backward. When you label those moments as "regression," it will inevitably create a sense of shame and only hinders your progress.

Let's say you've had a few weeks of feeling grounded, responsive, and balanced—and then something happens that triggers you, and it knocks you right back into your old patterns. It's okay. You haven't regressed, you haven't gone backward, and you haven't messed anything up. Every challenge you face is an opportunity to learn something new about yourself, your triggers, and your patterns. By approaching a perceived "regression" with a curious and open mindset, not only will you work through the trigger faster, you'll glean valuable insights that will inform your ongoing healing work.

JOURNAL PROMPTS FOR REFRAMING "REGRESSIONS" AS LESSONS

Use the following journaling prompts to work through your own thoughts and feelings about perceived regressions.

- Write about a time when you felt like you took a step backward in your healing journey. How did this make you feel? Did you notice any negative self-talk or self-judgment coming up?

- Imagine that you are looking back on this experience from the future, and write about how you might view it differently with hindsight. Can you see any lessons or insights that you will gain from this experience?

- Think about the skills or tools that you have learned on your healing journey so far. Are there any that you could use to help you navigate this setback? Write about how you might apply these skills in this situation.

- Consider what you might say to a friend who was going through a similar experience. How would you offer them support and encouragement? Now, write a letter to yourself in which you offer yourself that same support and encouragement.

- Reflect on the idea that setbacks are a normal and inevitable part of the healing process. Can you reframe this experience as an opportunity for growth and learning? Write about what you might do differently moving forward based on what you learned from this experience.

Striving for Perfection Only Creates Destruction

As a recovering perfectionist and a (quite stereotypical) Virgo, I learned the hard way that "perfect" progress doesn't exist. I fell into the perfectionist trap time and time again, expecting that I'd be able to undo decades of patterned anxiety in just a few short weeks. I put so much pressure on myself to grow quickly, not realizing that in doing so, I was actually just reinforcing the anxious patterns I wanted to heal from. Instead of celebrating any progress I had made, I would focus on everything I hadn't accomplished yet and shame the parts of me that still needed more healing.

My progress felt like it was two steps forward, two steps back until I was able to recognize and honor the truth that my pace was perfect, no matter how slow my ego deemed it to be. I was exactly where I needed to be, even if it was uncomfortable. The biggest lesson during my period of perceived "regressions" was about the importance of self-compassion: until I actually learned how to be more gentle and forgiving with myself, I'd keep coming back to the same sticking point.

Journal Prompts to Explore Your Perfectionist Tendencies

Use the following journaling prompts to examine your perfectionist tendencies and expand on how you can integrate more self-compassion throughout your journey.

- Have you ever experienced a time when your desire for perfection led to negative consequences? Describe the situation, and explain how you felt before, during, and after it.
- How do you define perfection? Where did this definition come from?
- How can you reframe perfection more compassionately? For example: "I will focus more on the process and my progress. I will do this by…"
- How has the pursuit of perfection affected your relationships with others? Have you ever felt that you needed to be perfect in order to be accepted or loved?
  - How will a more compassionate attitude toward yourself and your progress provide healing for those past experiences?
- What are some alternative ways to approach situations where you feel the pressure to be perfect? Reflect on any behavioral changes you can make or inner dialogue you can edit.
- How can you practice self-compassion and self-forgiveness when you make mistakes or fall short of your own expectations? What will you say to yourself? What can you remind yourself of?

So-Called "Failure" Is Usually Just a Growth Edge in Disguise

A growth edge is a point in your journey where you're on the cusp of a significant transformation. Often, someone will hit a growth edge when they're presented with an experience that feels overwhelming, and that overwhelm is presenting an opportunity to learn and evolve.

I remember when my client Justine was preparing to launch her first brick-and-mortar business. Justine had spent years selling her art online, but bringing her business into "real life" was a big, anxiety-inducing step for her. Despite her nerves, Justine was excited about her grand opening and hoped that it would be a huge success. She had poured her heart and soul into the business and was eager to share her creations with a wider audience.

However, when the day of the grand opening finally arrived, things didn't go as planned. Instead of the bustling crowd Justine had hoped for, barely any customers walked through the doors. Justine's anxiety skyrocketed. She began to worry about how she would be able to maintain rent and keep the store open if she didn't start getting more customers soon. Grand opening day seemed like a complete and total failure.

Justine's initial response to this disappointment was "Why is this happening to me?" but when she reframed it to "What is this growth edge asking of me?" everything changed. She was able to examine all of the reasons why this perceived failure might actually be a good thing. First, the situation presented her with an opportunity to challenge her limiting beliefs and fears about failure. Prior to the grand opening, Justine had been comfortable selling her art online, where she had control over her environment and could avoid the uncertainties and potential criticisms of face-to-face interactions. Launching a physical store required her to step out of her comfort zone and face the unknowns and potential risks of running a business in the real world.

This "failure" also illuminated where Justine could be running her business better. Prior to her grand opening, she hadn't spent much time thinking about marketing efforts, and that disappointing first day jump-started her ability to be resilient and resourceful. Justine had to adapt to the low foot traffic and brainstorm new, creative ways to generate interest and engagement with potential customers. She hadn't failed—she just hit a growth edge that challenged her to rise to the occasion and integrate the inner work she had been practicing. When she was able to reframe the perceived failure as a growth edge, Justine was able to approach her situation with curiosity, resiliency, and a deeper sense of empowerment. Within a few short days (and after a few adjustments to her marketing efforts), Justine was happily greeting customers at the door of her shop.

Growth edges often disguise themselves as failure. When you encounter a growth edge, do your best to approach it with curiosity and openness rather than fear or resistance. It may be tempting to retreat back to what feels safe and familiar, but staying in your comfort zone won't lead to growth. Instead, acknowledge the discomfort and lean into the challenge. You can remind yourself that growth edges are safe, normal, and good for you by using mantras or asking yourself questions. Here are a few examples.

- "It's not a setback, it's a setup!" Connect with how the perceived failure is setting you up to grow.
- "How is this working out for me right now?" A failure isn't something that happens to you—it happens *for* you.
- "Where's the growth?" Instead of focusing on the fall, find the opportunity to rise.
- "This is an adventure, not an obstacle." Lighten the energy. This perceived failure could actually be pointing you toward a more empowering path.

Chapter Reflections

Failure is an inevitable part of learning and growth. It allows you to learn from your mistakes, refine your approach, and double-down on your self-compassion and positive self-talk. Failing at something isn't proof that you're a failure; it's just presenting you with an opportunity to integrate your inner work and rise to the occasion. Sometimes you've gotta fail big to grow big! Use these journaling prompts to reflect on how you've historically responded to failure, and compassionately reframe those experiences as learnings.

- Can you think of a time when you experienced a setback or failure? What did you learn from that experience?
- What are some limiting beliefs you hold about yourself and failure? Develop an empowered replacement thought for each of the limiting beliefs you come up with.
- Reflect on situations in your healing and growth journey where you felt like you failed. In hindsight, how could you have been more compassionate with yourself? What can your previous experiences teach you about how to respond to failure in the future?
- In the future, how will you celebrate your successes and progress when things don't go as planned? What can you remind yourself of? How will you hype yourself back up?

Chapter Summary

Self-compassion is a requirement on your journey from anxiety to empowerment. Celebrate the wins, embrace growth edges, and make frequent stops along the way to smell the roses.

Chapter Ten
ENVISION AND EMBODY YOUR EMPOWERED SELF

Now that we've made it to the final chapter of this book, I'd like to point out something that you may have already realized. The truth is, you've had all of the empowerment you've needed within you all along. My hope is that now, having exercised your power through some pretty deep reflections and inner work, you'll give yourself permission to truly embody that power.

Embodiment is the process of fully integrating your empowered self into your thoughts, behaviors, and way of being. It's not just about having the vision or the ideas, but actively putting them into action in your everyday life. This means making intentional choices that align with your empowered self, even when it's uncomfortable or challenging. It means speaking up for yourself, setting boundaries, and working toward your goals. It means being kind and compassionate toward yourself, and giving yourself permission to make mistakes and learn from them. Embodiment is an ongoing process, and it requires consistent effort and commitment to yourself and your growth, but the rewards are immense. Living from a place of empowerment can bring you greater joy, more fulfillment, and a sense of purpose in your life. To embody your power is to integrate your learnings so that you can start living from the empowerment inside of you.

Envision Your Empowered Self

Now, the fun work begins. Allow yourself to tap into your Empowered Self by creating a clear picture of what that person looks like. You aren't just dreaming up a conceptual version of who you'd like to be—you're allowing a tangible expression of your empowerment to come forward.

You already have a vision of your Empowered Self deep within you, even if it's just a faint glimmer. In fact, it's the anxious part of you that's always been able to see the potential for empowerment; it's the part that was loudly signaling for you to pay attention. With the tools and self-understanding you've gained, you are now better equipped to envision and embrace your Empowered Self with more clarity and confidence. This is an exciting opportunity to step into your true potential and create a life filled with joy, empowerment, and self-love.

In this chapter, I will help you create a clear picture of your Empowered Self. As you read, it's important to remember that you're not creating an idealized version of yourself that is perfect in every way. Instead, you're envisioning a version of yourself that is fully empowered, aligned with your truest desires and values, and capable of navigating life's challenges with grace and confidence. This is a powerful process of self-discovery and growth, and it's essential to approach it with a sense of playfulness and curiosity. You might start to notice patterns in your thinking or behavior that have been holding you back, or you may discover new strengths and talents that you didn't even know you had.

As you begin to explore your Empowered Self, remember that this is a process, not a destination. There will be ups and downs along the way, and it's important to stay open to new experiences and ideas as they come. Check in with yourself regularly to assess how you're feeling and what you need to do to stay aligned with your vision. Above all, remember to have fun with this process! Your Empowered Self is a reflection of your highest potential, and by tapping into that energy, you can create a life that is truly fulfilling and full of joy. So don't be afraid to dream big and let your imagination run wild. The possibilities are truly limitless.

EXERCISE
Empowered Self Visioning Meditation

Before beginning this meditation, read through the instructions in full. Do your best to memorize them or record yourself reading the meditation and play it back. This way, you can fully engage in the practice and focus on your breath and inner experience rather than continuously referring to the book.

1. Begin by finding a comfortable position, either sitting or lying down. Take a few deep breaths in through your nose and out through your mouth, allowing your body to relax with each exhale.

2. Now, imagine a version of yourself who is confident and strong. This is your Empowered Self. Imagine them standing in front of you, radiating a warm and inviting energy. Take note of what they look like, what they're wearing, and their body language. How does their sense of empowerment manifest physically?

3. As you focus on this empowered version of yourself, begin to feel their energy flowing into your body. Feel yourself

becoming more confident, more capable, and more empowered with each passing moment.

4. Imagine that your Empowered Self is giving you a message. What do they want you to know? What advice do they have for you? Listen carefully and receive their guidance with an open heart and mind.

5. Now, take a moment to visualize yourself embodying this empowered version of yourself. See yourself moving through your day with confidence, strength, and ease. Notice how good it feels to be in this state of empowerment.

6. Take a deep breath in, and as you exhale, feel yourself fully integrating this energy of empowerment into your being. Know that you can access this Empowered Self at any time simply by connecting with this inner vision of yourself.

7. Take a few more deep breaths, and when you're ready, slowly open your eyes, feeling refreshed, rejuvenated, and empowered.

This is a meditation that I come back to often. It's such a great way to reconnect with your inherent sense of personal power and reset your perception of self.

Empowered Self Deep-Dive

In this section, I've shared a slew of prompts to help you define and connect with your Empowered Self from all angles. You will explore:

- Preparatory reflections, which will help you to create a conscious separation between your anxious inner dialogue and your Empowered Self inner dialogue.

- Feeling-based reflections, which are used to create clarity on the overall energy of your Empowered Self.
- Personality and lifestyle reflections, which are questions designed to bring your conceptual understanding of your Empowered Self into reality.

Read through the following questions. Select a few that resonate most, then respond to them in your journal. Answering three or four prompts is a great starting point. Over time, you can return to this list until you have answered each prompt.

PREPARATORY REFLECTIONS

- How is your Empowered Self different from your anxious inner voice?
- How do you know (feel) the difference between them?
- When you look at that difference, what practices seem most important for you to bolster?
- How can you respond to yourself when you feel stuck in your anxious inner voice and can't access your Empowered Self?

FEELING-BASED REFLECTIONS

- How does your Empowered Self feel about themselves? For example, do they feel strong, confident, or clear? Why?
- What makes them feel uniquely themselves?
- What is their energy like?
- What are their daily self-care practices? How do they honor themselves?
- How do they move through challenges?

- When they feel sadness, pain, anxiety, or anger, how do they respond?
- What do they journal about?
- What are they most grateful for?
- What are they most proud of?
- What are they most excited by, or excited about?

PERSONALITY AND LIFESTYLE REFLECTIONS

- What does your Empowered Self do for fun?
- How do they sound?
- How do they move, nourish, and/or otherwise support their body?
- How would their friends describe them?
- What value systems do they live their life by?
- What is their attitude toward [trigger]?
- What do they love to read? Watch? Listen to?
- Where do they live? Where would they like to live or visit frequently?
- How do they recharge physically? Emotionally?
- How do they honor their family, friendships, and partnerships?
- What are their spiritual practices?
- What are their boundaries? How do they express them?
- What is the quality of people in their life?
- What are their finances like? What is their relationship to money?
- How do they spend their free time?
- How do they give back to their community?

- How do they rest? How do they play?
- What is their favorite thing to eat? To wear? To do?
- How do they celebrate themselves?
- How do they celebrate others?

As you review and reflect on the answers to these questions, remember that feelings are the secret. Allow yourself to tap into the excitement and energy of your Empowered Self. Visualize yourself stepping into that version of you and feel the emotions that come with it. Let these feelings guide and motivate you as you work toward manifesting your Empowered Self in your daily life. Remember that your thoughts and emotions have a powerful impact on your reality, so keep cultivating the energy of your Empowered Self with positive thoughts and feelings.

Capture Your Empowered Self through an Essence Word

Another way to clarify who your Empowered Self is is by choosing an essence word. *Essence* is defined as "the most significant element, quality, or aspect of a thing or person."[22] Choosing an essence word is a powerful act of self-love, and it supports the claiming of who you truly are. It might be hard to boil it down to just one word (because, come on, your Empowered Self is pretty fantastic), but I'd like you to try. You might choose a personality descriptor like "bright," "adventurous," or "playful," or one that encapsulates the overall energy or state of mind of your Empowered Self.

---

22. *Merriam-Webster*, s.v. "essence (*n.*)," accessed September 27, 2023, https://www.merriam-webster.com/dictionary/essence.

An essence word is something you can anchor in to when you need to reconnect to your Empowered Self. Use your essence word as a neural reprogramming tool: think it, say it, breathe into it when you're need a reminder of who you are. This word also can serve as a fantastic visual aid; write it on sticky notes, add it to your vision board, or display it as your smart phone's wallpaper. Rest assured, your essence word doesn't have to be the same for life. It might be something to revisit during major milestones like birthdays or New Year's Day.

There's no "wrong" way to work with your essence word. If you have access to arts and crafts materials (such as colored pencils, paper, markers, or scrapbooking materials), it's always fun to activate your essence word through intentional, conscious creativity. Throw on some of your favorite feel-good songs, grab some supplies, and make something that reflects who your Empowered Self is. Turn your essence word into art in whatever way feels right for you. It can be as simple as writing it down on a blank piece of paper or as detailed as creating a full-sized vision board with your essence word at the very center. If you're feeling unsure of how to begin, here are a few creativity prompts.

- How would you draw, color, or paint your essence word?
- How big would your word be?
- Would it be big and bold? Clean and soft? Beautifully chaotic?
- What tools, textures, or materials would help communicate the essence or vibe of your Empowered Self? For example, if your Empowered Self is soft yet strong, you might incorporate textures like silk or satin to represent the softness, or use materials like clay or texture paste to represent the strength they have built.

Find Your Empowered Self by Reversing Your "I Wish" Statements

Your Empowered Self has been trying to make an appearance for a while, and you can look to your thoughts for clues about how they want to show up. Pay attention to your language too. For example, if you find yourself saying "I wish I could start my own business," try changing it to "I will start my own business." This simple shift can help you tap into your Empowered Self and take action toward your goal. Similarly, if you find yourself saying "I want to take a pottery class one day," try changing it to "I am going to take a pottery class this week." Speaking in the present tense will encourage you to take action on your desires.

The important thing, of course, is to follow through! If you really do want to take a pottery class, book the lesson. If you plan to start your own business, set aside an hour this month to actually work on your business plan. You don't have to do everything all at once, but focusing on—and executing—the first or next step will help you to maintain momentum. Action is what takes your vision and turns it into embodiment.

Embody Your Empowerment; Be Them Now

All that's left for you to do now is begin to embody that beautiful vision of yours. Be that person—now.

You are already ready. You don't have to wait until you trust yourself more, or you feel more confident, or whatever reason you're using to believe you're not ready. Trust that your readiness and your confidence are already enough. You wouldn't have been able to envision an empowered version of yourself if you weren't ready to step into it.

I remember when a former teacher of mine first introduced the concept of "be them now." I was in the beginning stages of building my coaching practice while working a full-time job and teaching yoga classes on the side. I felt overwhelmed, and my time was stretched so thin that I started to fear that I would never be ready to coach full-time. There was so much I still had to do! I needed to save enough money to quit my nine to five, create a client base, learn how to file my taxes as a business owner, create a marketing plan—the list went on. There were so many tangible steps that I hadn't yet taken, and it scared me. I started thinking I'd never be ready to transition into the life I'd been envisioning. When I shared my concerns with my teacher, they said to me, "Amanda, none of those things have anything to do with being a coach. Just be a coach now. Be her now."

Easy for you to say, I thought. But when I plied my teacher for more information on what they meant by "be her now," I started to realize that they were encouraging me to step into the mindset and energy of my Empowered Self as a coach even before I felt entirely "ready." They were asking me to simply make the decision that I already was a coach and business owner, and to let that mindset fuel how I handled my next steps. This shift in perspective allowed me to approach problem-solving and decision-making with newfound self-trust and confidence.

Stepping into the role of a coach before all the boxes were checked expanded my horizons and showed me a world of possibilities beyond my initial fears. In the process, I felt liberated, and I noticed my passion for coaching grow even more. The concept of "be them now" had taken root in my journey, paving the way for a transformation that surpassed my wildest expectations.

There a lot of ways to label this work: quantum jumping, timeline shifting, even manifestation. Regardless of the label you choose, the work is still the same: it's a choice to step into a new you—and, of course, a belief that it's possible. Deciding to live as the empowered version of yourself now doesn't mean that you are without your current life circumstances. It just means you start showing up in your life differently.

So, really, why not be that person now?

Faith It 'til You Make It

The popular saying "fake it 'til you make it" suggests pretending or acting as if you're already successful or confident in a certain area of life, even if you may not feel that way initially. By behaving in a way that reflects the desired outcome, the idea is that you will eventually internalize those behaviors and beliefs, leading to an actual sense of success or confidence. The approach isn't wrong, but the word *fake* never really resonated with me. *Fake* implies that there's something disingenuous about your process, like you're trying to become someone or something else and hoping you don't get caught. That, my friends, is not the vibe we're going for with this work.

Instead of "fake it 'til you make it," try "faith it 'til you make it" on for size. I like to think of this saying as you simply investing faith in who you are becoming. You're claiming that version of yourself now, holding the belief that you will grow into your vision. You're investing faith in who you are becoming. When you're acting as if you already are your Empowered Self, you're not being fake; you're channeling the energy and mindset that a future version of yourself already has. It's about having faith in your ability to create the reality you want and trusting that you have everything you need within you to make it happen. It's about stepping into your power and living from a place of intention, rather than just going through the motions and hoping for the best. As long as you're aligning your thoughts, feelings, and actions with that vision of yourself, there's nothing "fake" about it.

I do want to acknowledge how strange, or even scary, it might seem to just start showing up as a new version of you. It can sound like you're pulling the whole "fake it 'til you make it" thing, but you're not. There is nothing fake about you deciding to embody a version of yourself that you have created. If your Empowered Self vision came from you—and if it feels good, exciting, and safe when you think about it—it's yours. It's right for you. It *is* you.

Empowerment Is Your Birthright

I want you to say the following sentence out loud, and say it with as much authenticity as you can muster: "I deserve to live a happy, vibrant, and empowered life." Pay attention to how it feels when you say a statement like that aloud. Notice how your voice sounds, which emotions come up, and if you truly believe the words you're saying.

You weren't put on this planet to live an anxious or disempowered life. You are a brilliant, beautiful soul inhabiting a body, and your true nature is one of joy, well-being, and empowerment. I know that might be hard to believe at times, especially when you're battling waves of anxiety, but your anxiety is not a reflection of your true nature. To truly embody the statement "I deserve to live a happy, healthy, and empowered life," you must examine your limiting beliefs.

Limiting Beliefs

Limiting beliefs are systems of thought that restrict, hinder, or limit your ability to dream bigger or expect better for yourself. These don't necessarily have to be thoughts that you speak out loud; limiting beliefs are often quiet, inner assumptions that have been formed through various experiences, conditioning, and societal norms.

By taking the time to reflect on your thoughts and beliefs, you will be able to identify and challenge what has been unconsciously limiting you. Here are some examples of common limiting beliefs.

"I Don't Deserve to Be Happy in More than One Area of My Life"

Beliefs such as this one impose a restriction on your ability to experience happiness in multiple areas of life. This belief suggests that happiness is limited or restricted to only one aspect, which can result in a self-imposed limitation on your overall well-being and fulfillment. Not everything will be perfect all the time, but you deserve to have a general sense of joy in various areas of your life.

"I'm Not Smart/Talented/Skilled Enough"

This belief can lead to a negative self-perception and a lack of confidence in your abilities, resulting in self-limiting behavior and missed opportunities for growth and empowerment. Chances are, this is a story stemming from self-worth. But, let's say you actually don't have the skills to do something yet—that doesn't mean you can't, or won't, learn how to do it.

"I'm Too Old/Young to Achieve My Dreams"

Age is just a number, baby. Thinking you're too old or too young to do something will only lead to missed opportunities. Celebrate your age, whatever it is, as well as your unique perspectives and experiences that come with it.

"If Someone Is Upset with Me, I Can't Be Happy"

Limiting beliefs like this one stem from people-pleasing tendencies and can cause you to neglect your needs and desires. Hold this duality: you can be happy while another person has their own emotional experience.

"Success Is Only for Lucky or Special People"

This belief is riddled with unworthiness. Who says you're not a special or lucky person?!

———

It's important to remember that your limiting beliefs are not set in stone, and you have the power to change them. Embracing the truth that you deserve to live a happy, healthy, and empowered life starts with addressing your limiting beliefs.

Now that you've examined the subconscious limits unique to you, it's time to start telling a better story! Replace them with empowering beliefs that align with your true nature and potential. When you release the shackles of your limiting beliefs, you begin to see yourself and the world in a new light. You realize that you are capable of achieving greatness, and that you deserve to live a life full of joy. You start to trust your own abilities and intuition, and you make authentic choices. You become your Empowered Self.

Chapter Reflections

In your journal, make a list of the limiting beliefs you hold about yourself. Be sure to explore all facets of your belief systems. Identify where you limit yourself in your power, your potential, your ability to give and receive love, your success, and even your finances. Then, reflect on the following prompts.

- Are these beliefs based on facts or assumptions? Are they helping you or holding you back? Why?

- Now, challenge the limiting beliefs you've held about yourself and your capabilities by coming up with empowered thoughts that counteract them. For each limiting belief, write down at least two empowering affirmations or thoughts to replace them with.

- Recall a past success or achievement that you feel proud of. How did you overcome any limiting beliefs or self-doubt to achieve that success? Reflect on the inner strength and determination you exhibited during that time.

- Imagine yourself as a marathon runner on the path from anxiety to empowerment. Along this journey, where are the moments you think you will need the most encouragement and celebration? Write about the types of support and encouragement you may need at different points along your journey.

- Practice self-compassion on this journey. Acknowledge that transformation takes time, and there may be moments of setback or doubt. How can you celebrate and show kindness to yourself, regardless of where you are on the path to empowerment?

- Visualize your future self living a life free from the limitations of anxiety. Describe the empowering thoughts and beliefs that guide your actions and decisions in this empowered state. How does this version of you approach challenges and embrace opportunities for growth?

Chapter Summary

You are, and have always been, filled with power. Recognize that. Celebrate that. You deserve to bask in appreciation for yourself, even if you feel like you're "not there yet," or you still have a way to go on your journey. Have you ever watched a marathon? There's a reason people don't only congregate at the finish line. Crowds of supporters—family, friends, strangers—gather all along the course to cheer on runners at different points. People gather with signs of encouragement like "Keep going!" and "Proud of you!" to celebrate and encourage the journey itself. Your journey from anxiety to empowerment deserves every last ounce of celebration and encouragement too.

CONCLUSION

Congratulations, dear reader. You've made it to the end of this book, which means you've gone through a hell of a lot of inner work. Through the journal prompts, somatic exercises, and actionable insights, you've begun managing your anxiety and paving your own path toward growth. I hope this process has shown you how powerful, capable, and worthy you truly are. You've invested time, effort, and courage into exploring new ways to manage anxiety and create a more empowered life, and that's worth celebrating! You've done quite a bit of writing and reflection throughout our time together, but don't close that journal just yet—this point in your life deserves some dedicated reflection too.

Reflecting on your progress and celebrating yourself is a crucial aspect of your continued empowerment. Acknowledging your achievements, both big and small, reinforces your relationship with Self and motivates you to keep moving forward. It's a way to honor the effort, resilience, and determination you have put into your journey, and it serves as a reminder of how far you have come.

As you reach the end of this book, I invite you to take a moment to go back and reread the letter you wrote to yourself. (Remember that?) Reflect on the emotions that arise as you read your own words of love, commitment, and dedication to your healing. Notice how far you've come on your journey and the progress you've made in deepening your relationship with yourself. Allow yourself to feel the emotions that arise, whether you feel joy, gratitude, a sense of empowerment, or something else. Then, take this opportunity to acknowledge and celebrate your growth and progress. Recognize the love and compassion you have for yourself and the strength and resilience you've shown throughout this journey. Your letter is a powerful reminder of your worth and the unwavering commitment you have made to your own healing.

After reading through your original self-love letter, take a moment to sit with these final reflections.

- When you first began this journey, how did you feel? What was your relationship with your Self? How did your body feel, and what was the quality of your thoughts?

- How do you feel now, compared to back then? Remember, this is not about comparison or perfection, but about appreciating your unique journey and growth.

- What tools, exercises, or learnings were the most helpful for you? Take note of the techniques that really resonated.

- What are you most proud of when it comes to your journey? What did you learn about yourself? What have been your biggest wins? What deserves some celebration?

- Knowing what you know now, what would you tell younger versions of yourself? Would you tell them how you know that you'll be okay? Would you offer yourself words of encouragement? Let this reflection be healing for all parts of you.

As you move forward, remember to continue nurturing the relationship with yourself. Keep practicing self-care, self-compassion, and self-empowerment. Embrace all that you've learned, and continue to integrate it in your daily life. Trust in your own wisdom and know that you have the ability to continue healing and growing, one step at a time.

Throughout these pages, you've learned valuable tools and insights that can help you navigate the challenges of anxiety with greater awareness and resilience. You've explored a wide array of topics, ranging from basic anxiety management tools to deeper work around emotional processes, ownership, and empower-ment. You've read a *lot* of information, and I want to remind you that this book is not meant to be a one-time read—it's a tool you can refer back to whenever you need it. Reread the sections that resonated with you, explore the journal prompts in more depth, or revisit any of the meditations as needed.

I want to express my own gratitude to you for embarking on this journey from anxiety to empowerment. I commend your dedication, courage, and commitment to yourself. You are—and always have been—capable of creating positive change in your life, and I deeply believe in your ability to create a fulfilling, empowered life. Keep going, and trust that you have what it takes to thrive.

Oh, one more thing.

In case nobody's told you lately…

I love you, and I'm so very, very proud of you.

Congratulations!

RESOURCES

Welcome to the resources section, a treasure trove of valuable tools and recommending reading, carefully curated to compliment and enhance your journey from anxiety to empowerment. This resources section may be a bit more in-depth than other books' resources sections; don't skip this part!

The recommending reading is presented in chapter-by-chapter format: if certain chapters in this book resonated strongly for you, I suggest checking out the reading recommendations for that chapter first to compliment the inner work you're feeling called to. You'll also find free warmline and hotline information and resources for substance abuse.

Resources by Chapter

Each chapter in this book delves into various concepts and practices to support anxiety management, emotional healing, and personal growth. The resources listed in this section build on the material discussed in each chapter, and will serve to further support your transformation. From insightful books and research to practical tools, these resources are is designed to provide you with a diverse range of materials to continue your path toward empowerment and well-being.

CHAPTER 1

Opening the Door of Your Heart: And Other Buddhist Tales of Happiness by Ajahn Brahm

This was one of my favorite books to read early on in my anxiety management journey. The inspiring, healing, and joyful stories Ajahn Brahm relays offer a deep sense of perspective and inner grace.

I Thought It Was Just Me (But It Isn't): Making the Journey from "What Will People Think?" to "I Am Enough" by Brené Brown

This book shines a long-overdue light on an important truth: our imperfections are what connect us to one another and to our humanity. A must-read for the anxious-minded person who feels alone in their journey.

Accessing the Healing Power of the Vagus Nerve: Self-Help Exercises for Anxiety, Depression, Trauma, and Autism by Stanley Rosenberg

Through a series of easy self-help exercises, the book illustrates the simple ways you can regulate the vagus nerve in order to initiate deep relaxation and improve your emotional well-being.

Activate Your Vagus Nerve: Unleash Your Body's Natural Ability to Heal by Dr. Navaz Habib

Packed with easy-to-follow exercises and activities, this book shows you how to unlock the power of the vagus nerve to heal your body and get back to a state of balance.

To learn more about the relationship between the heart and brain, here are a few great resources.

- **The HeartMath Institute:** The HeartMath Institute has developed fantastic, scientifically validated tools that I use with my own clients to help them regulate stress and increase their sense of emotional security. I recommend visiting their website to explore their free tools and trainings. You can also visit their research library here: www .heartmath.org/research/research-library.

- **The National Institute of Health:** There's a wealth of information available that offers a more clinical understanding of the vagus nerve. Read just one of the studies here: www .ncbi.nlm.nih.gov/pmc/articles/PMC9093220.

CHAPTER 2

Llewellyn's Complete Book of Chakras: Your Definitive Source of Energy Center Knowledge for Health, Happiness, and Spiritual Evolution by Cyndi Dale

The Complete Book of Chakra Healing is a fantastic resource to help you integrate the powerful forces of your energy body into your everyday life for better health, increased happiness and creativity, and a stronger awareness of your life's true purpose. Cyndi is one of my biggest mentors and is a wealth of information.

Healing Ourselves: Biofield Science and the Future of Health by Shamini Jain

Dr. Jain is a brilliant, passionate, and well-researched force of nature who presents an integrated path to healing and empowerment. In *Healing Ourselves*, Shamini presents a perspective that connects science and spirituality. Her peer-reviewed research on biofield science explores the inseparable relationship between consciousness and healing. The book also offers in-depth instruction with evidence-based recommendations on spiritual practices that can be used in your life for healing.

Wheels of Life: A User's Guide to the Chakra System by Anodea Judith

This book is my chakra "Bible," and it is a great option for those who are brand new to the world of energy centers. *Wheels of Life* has all of the need-to-know information about each chakra, and it is complete with meditations, tools, and exercises to help you start working with your chakras. Along with gaining spiritual wisdom, you'll experience better health, more energy, enhanced creativity, and the ability to manifest your dreams.

Loving What Is: Four Questions that Can Change Your Life by Byron Katie

This book offers a framework of four simple questions that, when applied to a specific problem, enable you to see what is troubling you in an entirely different light. If the "truth versus story" exercise in chapter 2 was helpful for you, *Loving What Is* will take that exploration deeper.

Energy Anatomy: The Science of Personal Power, Spirituality, and Health by Caroline Myss

This was one of the first spiritual books I picked up when I started my healing journey. It's a transformative exploration of the human energy system, delving into the intricate connections between mind, body, and spirit, and providing invaluable insights into the power and influence of energetic anatomy on overall well-being. This book is a bit heady, but don't be intimidated. I've found it's one of those books that calls to you when you need it—you might read a few chapters and not come back to it for a while. But when you do, it always seems to be at the perfect time.

Here are a few more resources for the tools covered in this chapter.

- **Weighted Blankets:** To learn more about the somatic benefits of weighted blankets, visit www.pubmed.ncbi.nlm.nih.gov/32204779. My favorite weighted blanket is the Gravity Blanket, which can be found at www.gravityblankets.com. Online retailers have a wealth of budget-friendly options.
- **Online Yoga:** You don't need to spend an arm and a leg to develop a fantastic, nourishing yoga practice. YouTube has a plethora of free resources! Use search terms such as "yoga nidra," "anxiety-reducing yoga flow," or "yin yoga."
- **Emotional Freedom Technique (EFT) Tapping:** To learn more about EFT Tapping, visit www.eftinternational.org.

CHAPTER 3

The Sleep Solution: Why Your Sleep Is Broken and How to Fix It by W. Chris Winter

In this book, Dr. Winter shares what he's learned about the science of sleeping after helping over ten thousand patients get better rest. His goal is to teach people how to get the best night of sleep possible without the aid of sleeping pills. He dives deep into exploring the root cause of what's keeping you up at night so that you can enjoy restful shut-eye.

Why We Sleep: Unlocking the Power of Sleep and Dreams by Matthew Walker

Why We Sleep is a great read to affirm the importance of sleep and understand how it affects the brain, enriches our ability to learn, recalibrates emotions, restocks the immune system, and more. Walker is the Director of UC Berkeley's Sleep and Neuroimaging Lab, so the data and suggestions in this book are both effective and backed by science.

Here is a bit more information on a few of the tools and resources mentioned in chapter 3.

- **Binaural Beats:** Most major music-streaming platforms have free, sleep-focused binaural beat tracks available. I recommend searching Spotify for "binaural beats for sleep" playlists. There are dozens of premade playlists to choose from that are long enough to last you through the night. Many YouTube creators also offer binaural beats support. To learn more about the positive benefits of binaural beats for sleep (and a slew of other tips and resources on sleep health), visit www.sleepfoundation.org/noise-and-sleep /binaural-beats.

- **NSDR:** To learn more about Andrew Huberman's perspective on Non-Sleep Deep Rest (yoga nidra), visit www.nsdr.co.

Chapter 4

Codependent No More: How to Stop Controlling Others and Start Caring for Yourself by Melody Beattie

This book is a wonderful lesson in boundary-setting and emotional regulation, taught through the lens of codependency. Whether or not you identify as a codependent person, this book is chock-full of lessons and exercises that will help strengthen your ability to set boundaries and show up authentically for yourself.

Energetic Boundaries: How to Stay Protected and Connected in Work, Love, and Life by Cyndi Dale

This book is a fantastic resource for those seeking an understanding of boundaries on the energetic level. Just as our physical body is protected by our skin, our psyche and spirit have energetic boundaries that keep out harmful influences. These "spiritual borders" are our soul's way of communicating to the universe what we do and don't want to experience in life.

The Set Boundaries Workbook: Practical Exercises for Understanding Your Needs and Setting Healthy Limits by Nedra Glover Tawwab

This book is an engaging, accessible, step-by-step resource for setting, communicating, and enforcing healthy boundaries at home, at work, and in life. If you enjoyed the written components of my book, this *Set Boundaries Workbook* might be right up your alley.

CHAPTER 5

Rise Sister Rise: A Guide to Unleashing the Wise, Wild Woman Within by Rebecca Campbell

This book was one of the most validating, life-changing books for me in my own spiritual and emotional healing journey. This book is a call to arms for the sacred feminine to rise up, heal insecurities, tell the truth, and lead from our own inner wisdom.

You Are the Universe: Discovering Your Cosmic Self and Why It Matters by Deepak Chopra and Menas Kafatos

You Are the Universe literally means what it says: each of us is a co-creator of reality extending to the vastest reaches of time and space. This book is a beautiful, easy-to-digest understanding of the infinite nature of our being.

The Seat of the Soul by Gary Zukav

This book is a spiritual classic that delves into the power of the soul and how it can guide us toward authentic fulfillment and spiritual growth. I recommend reading this book if you'd like to dive deeper into your own embodiment work.

The Artist's Way: A Spiritual Path to Higher Creativity by Julia Cameron

An absolutely fantastic book to help people develop soulful self-understanding. While primarily focused on creativity, this book helps you connect with your inner self and embrace spiritual growth. I also enjoyed the accountability factor of this book; there are daily and weekly reflections and activities for you to complete that will keep you engaged in your self-development.

CHAPTER 6

The 7 Habits of Highly Effective People: Powerful Lessons in Personal Change by Stephen R. Covey

This classic book offers timeless principles that empower individuals to achieve personal and professional success through self-awareness and proactive habits.

Unfu*k Yourself: Get Out of Your Head and into Your Life by Gary John Bishop

Bishop takes a no-nonsense approach and explains how to break free from self-limiting beliefs and embrace self-empowerment and positive change.

Atomic Habits: An Easy & Proven Way to Build Good Habits & Break Bad Ones by James Clear

Atomic Habits presents practical strategies to create lasting habits and transform your life through the power of small, intentional actions.

CHAPTER 7

The Body Keeps the Score: Brain, Mind, and Body in the Healing of Trauma by Bessel van der Kolk

Dr. van der Kolk, a leading expert on trauma, explores the profound impact of trauma on the brain and body and offers effective treatments for healing. This book is an affirming and insightful read for those who have experienced trauma and are continuing to heal from it.

The Post-Traumatic Growth Guidebook: Practical Mind-Body Tools to Heal Trauma, Foster Resilience, and Awaken Your Potential by Arielle Schwartz

This guidebook offers practical exercises and tools to promote post-traumatic growth and resilience in the aftermath of trauma.

Healing Developmental Trauma: How Early Trauma Affects Self-Regulation, Self-Image, and the Capacity for Relationship by Laurence Heller and Aline LaPierre

The authors explore the impact of early developmental trauma and how it can manifest in adulthood, including anxiety-triggering patterns.

It Didn't Start with You: How Inherited Family Trauma Shapes Who We Are and How to End the Cycle by Mark Wolynn

The author explores the intergenerational transmission of trauma and provides insight into breaking the cycle. If you enjoyed the inner child work in this book, *It Didn't Start with You* is an excellent next step.

Chapter 8

The Biology of Belief: Unleashing the Power of Consciousness, Matter & Miracles by Bruce H. Lipton

I love Dr. Lipton's work. Originally a skeptic of consciousness and spirituality, his own research into new biology radically shifted his understanding of what it means to be human. *The Biology of Belief* explores how our thoughts and beliefs contribute to the health of our cells—and life as a whole.

Breaking the Habit of Being Yourself: How to Lose Your Mind and Create a New One by Joe Dispenza

Dr. Dispenza's work has had a profound impact on my own life, and this book was the start of it all. In *Breaking the Habit of Being Yourself*, Dr. Dispenza (a neuroscientist, chiropractor, and renowned teacher in the field of personal development and consciousness) explores the power of the mind and provides practical techniques to break free from self-limiting patterns and habits. He delves into the science of neuroplasticity, explaining how our brains can be rewired to create positive change. The book offers valuable insight into the mind-body connection and empowers readers to transform their lives by changing their thoughts, emotions, and actions.

Letting Go: The Pathway of Surrender by David R. Hawkins

This is an excellent choice for someone struggling to let go of emotional pain, whether it stems from a breakup, a traumatic incident, or another experience from the past. This book explores the concept of surrender as a means to achieve inner peace and higher states of consciousness. In *Letting Go*, Dr. Hawkins (a renowned psychiatrist, spiritual teacher, and author) delves into the process of releasing negative emotions and attachments to attain profound spiritual and emotional freedom.

Feeling Is the Secret by Neville Goddard

In this transformative book, Goddard emphasizes the power of our emotions and beliefs in manifesting our desires. He reveals how our inner states—particularly the feelings we hold in our hearts—create the external circumstances of our lives. By aligning our thoughts and feelings with the reality we wish to experience, we can consciously attract positive outcomes and live a more fulfilling life. This book is a fantastic support for the "firelog memories" concept discussed in chapter 8.

CHAPTER 9

*Buy Yourself the F*cking Lilies: And Other Rituals to Fix Your Life* by Tara Schuster

This is a fun, easy, and empowering read for anyone who might be struggling with self-love. Schuster offers a refreshing perspective on personal growth and navigating life's challenges with resilience and grace. In a blend of memoir and self-help, Schuster's book reads like a friend who is sharing her journey of healing and self-discovery with you.

Rising Strong: How the Ability to Reset Transforms the Way We Live, Love, Parent, and Lead by Brené Brown

This was one of the most transformative books I read in my early twenties, and it's one of my most-recommended books to clients. Dr. Brown shares how vulnerability and resilience contribute to personal empowerment and the ability to envision a more fulfilling life. Reading her books feels like receiving a warm hug when you need it most; you'll feel supported, validated, and inspired to keep going.

The Power of Now: A Guide to Spiritual Enlightenment by Eckhart Tolle

Tolle's work can be summarized as simple spiritual wisdom that transcends the complexity of modern-day living. This transformative book explores the importance of living in the present moment and embracing the power of now to create a vision for an empowered future. Whenever I read Tolle, I'm reminded that simplicity is often best.

CHAPTER 10

You Are a Badass: How to Stop Doubting Your Greatness and Start Living an Awesome Life by Jen Sincero

This empowering book encourages you to embrace your inner power, unleash your potential, and manifest the life you've been dreaming of. Sincero is a wildly engaging author, and her words were a huge catalyst for my own mindset transformation. I used to refer to this book as a "sneaky spirituality" (in a good way!) because Sincero does such a great job of introducing spiritual truths and tools without sounding preachy or woo-woo.

The Art of Extraordinary Confidence: Your Ultimate Path to Love, Wealth, and Freedom by Aziz Gazipura

Gazipura presents a transformative guide to breaking free from social anxiety and self-doubt to achieve lasting confidence. With his expertise in clinical psychology and a warm, engaging writing style, Dr. Gazipura offers practical techniques and powerful mindset shifts that empower readers to navigate social situations with ease, embrace their authentic selves, and build unshakable confidence. This book is a valuable resource for anyone looking to overcome insecurities and develop a more confident mindset.

May Cause Miracles: A 40-Day Guidebook of Subtle Shifts for Radical Change and Unlimited Happiness by Gabrielle Bernstein

Bernstein presents a forty-day guide to shift perceptions and create profound positive change in daily life. Drawing from principles of *A Course in Miracles* by Helen Schucman (another fantastic read), Bernstein offers practical, spiritual exercises that aim to dissolve fear, release negative thought patterns, and cultivate a deeper connection to love and inner peace. Through daily reflections, meditations, and affirmations, readers embark on a transformative journey that can lead to a miraculous shift in their thoughts, relationships, and overall well-being. *May Cause Miracles* is a powerful and accessible guide for those seeking to embrace a more empowered, loving, and miraculous life.

The Desire Map: A Guide to Creating Goals with Soul by Danielle LaPorte

This book helps readers connect with their core desired feelings to create empowering visions and set goals that align with their authentic selves. If you've never resonated with more traditional goal-setting structures (like SMART goals or the PACT method), this book might be more in alignment with you. Instead of leading with the mind (the way traditional goal setting methods do), *The Desire Map* encourages you to lead first with the spirit.

Resources for Those with an Anxious Attachment Style

In my years of working as a coach, one of the most common things I work on with my clients is anxious attachment style work. If you resonate with an anxious attachment style, you are certainly not alone in your journey. Understanding and navigating attachment styles can be a transformative process, and having additional resources at your disposal can provide valuable insights and support along the way. The following recommended reading materials delve into the intricacies of anxious attachment and offer practical strategies to cultivate healthier connections with yourself and others.

Attached: The New Science of Adult Attachment and How It Can Help You Find—and Keep—Love by Amir Levine and Rachel S. F. Heller

This book delves into the science of adult attachment styles, offering valuable insights and guidance on forming and maintaining healthy relationships.

Insecure in Love: How Anxious Attachment Can Make You Feel Jealous, Needy, and Worried and What You Can Do about It by Leslie Becker-Phelps

This book explores the impact of anxious attachment on romantic relationships and provides practical strategies to address and overcome insecurity.

Avoidant: How to Love (or Leave) a Dismissive Partner by Jeb Kinnison

While primarily focused on avoidant attachment, this book offers a comprehensive understanding of attachment styles and how they can interact in relationships.

Wired for Love: How Understanding Your Partner's Brain and Attachment Style Can Help You Defuse Conflict and Build a Secure Relationship by Stan Tatkin

Dr. Tatkin combines neuroscience and attachment theory to help couples build more secure and fulfilling relationships.

Love Me Don't Leave Me: Overcoming Fear of Abandonment & Building Lasting, Loving Relationships by Michelle Skeen

This is a powerful and insightful guide that explores the realm of fears and insecurities that arise from abandonment issues.

Through practical exercises and compassionate wisdom, this book offers valuable tools to help individuals heal old wounds, develop healthier relationship patterns, and embrace a more secure and fulfilling approach to love and intimacy.

Mr. Unavailable and the Fallback Girl: The Definitive Guide to Understanding Emotionally Unavailable Men and the Women that Love Them by Natalie Lue

Lue provides a candid and eye-opening exploration of the dynamics between emotionally unavailable partners and those who find themselves repeatedly drawn to them. With a blend of humor and compassion, this book helps readers break free from unhealthy patterns, gain clarity on their own worth, and cultivate stronger boundaries to create healthier and more fulfilling relationships.

The Attachment Theory Workbook: Powerful Tools to Promote Understanding, Increase Stability, and Build Lasting Relationships by Annie Chen

This workbook provides actionable exercises and strategies to help individuals cultivate healthier attachment patterns.

Mental Health Resources

Navigating life's challenges and seeking support during difficult times is an essential part of the journey to growth and healing. Whether you're facing mental health concerns, struggling with addiction, or seeking a supportive community, these resources offer a safe space for you to connect with others who have shared experiences. Remember, reaching out for support is a sign of strength, and there is no shame in seeking help. These resources are here to empower you and remind you that you are not alone.

Let's explore these invaluable resources together, providing a bridge toward hope, healing, and a brighter tomorrow.

If you or someone you know is struggling with their mental health, help is readily available at any of the following mental health and crisis resources. Please note that these resources were up-to-date at the time of publication, though they may have changed.

RESOURCES FOR READERS IN THE UNITED STATES OF AMERICA

Crisis hotlines and "warmlines" both provide support and assistance to individuals in times of need, but they serve different purposes and characteristics. Crisis hotlines are typically designed to help individuals who are experiencing a mental health crisis, emotional distress, or an immediate and severe crisis situation. Warmlines, on the other hand, are generally intended for those who may be experiencing non-emergency emotional distress, loneliness, or isolation but are not in an acute crisis.

Warmlines
National Alliance of Mental Illness (NAMI)
Phone: 1-800-950-6264
Website: www.nami.org

For additional warmline resources, including resources by state, visit www.warmline.org.

Hotlines
National Suicide Prevention Lifeline
Phone: Call 988
Website: www.988lifeline.org

Crisis Text Line
Phone: Text "HOME" to 741741
Website: www.crisistextline.org

Mental Health America
Phone: Call 1-800-985-5990 (Disaster Distress Helpline)
Website: www.mhanational.org

The Trevor Project
Phone: Call 1-866-488-7386
Website: www.thetrevorproject.org

Substance Abuse and Mental Health Services Administration (SAMHSA) National Helpline
Phone: Call 1-800-662-HELP (1-800-662-4357)
Website: www.samhsa.gov/find-help/national-helpline

Rape, Abuse & Incest National Network (RAINN) Sexual Assault Hotline
Phone: Call 1-800-656-HOPE (1-800-656-4673)
Website: www.rainn.org

RESOURCES FOR READERS IN THE UNITED KINGDOM

Samaritans
Phone: Call 116 123 (Freephone)
Website: www.samaritans.org

Crisis Text Line
Phone: Text "SHOUT" to 85258
Website: www.giveusashout.org

RESOURCES FOR READERS IN AUSTRALIA
Lifeline
Phone: Call 13 11 14
Website: www.lifeline.org.au

Beyond Blue
Phone: Call 1300 22 4636
Website: www.beyondblue.org.au

RESOURCES FOR READERS IN CANADA
Crisis hotlines and "warmlines" both provide support and assistance to individual in times of need, but they serve different purposes and characteristics. Crisis hotlines are typically designed to help individuals who are experiencing a mental health crisis, emotional distress, or an immediate and severe crisis situation. Warmlines, on the other hand, are generally intended for those who may be experiencing non-emergency emotional distress, loneliness, or isolation but are not in an acute crisis.

Warmlines
Mental Health Peer Support
Phone: 416-960-9267
Website: www.warmline.ca

Hope for Wellness Helpline (Indigenous Services Canada)
Phone: 1-855-242-3310
Website: www.hopeforwellness.ca

Hotlines
Talk Suicide Canada
Phone: 1-833-456-4566
Website: www.talksuicide.ca

Crisis Centre of BC
Phone: 1-800-784-2433
Website: www.crisiscentre.bc.ca

Crisis Text Line
Phone: Text "CONNECT" to 686868
Website: www.crisistextline.ca

Please note that these helplines are not a substitute for professional medical or mental health treatment. If you or someone you know is in immediate danger or experiencing a medical emergency, please call emergency services or visit your nearest hospital. Reaching out for support is a powerful step toward healing, and there are caring individuals ready to listen and support you through difficult times. Remember, you are not alone on this journey, and there are brighter days ahead.

Free Therapy Resources in the United States

Accessing therapy and mental health support should not be limited by financial barriers. If you or someone you know is in need of mental health resources but cannot afford traditional therapy, there are free or low-cost options available. Here is a list of free therapy resources in the United States that offer various services to support your mental well-being.

Open Path
Website: www.openpathcollective.org
Open Path Psychotherapy Collective connects clients with mental health professionals who offer affordable, sliding-scale fees between thirty and seventy dollars per session.

7 Cups
Website: www.7cups.com
7 Cups provides free online emotional support through trained active listeners. They also offer low-cost online therapy with licensed therapists.

Free 12-Step Programs in the United States

For individuals seeking support in overcoming addiction or other behavioral challenges, 12-step programs have been a valuable resource. These programs provide a supportive community, guidance, and a structured approach to recovery. If you or someone you know is looking for a 12-step program to address addiction or other issues, here is a list of some well-known 12-step programs available in the United States. Each program offers a safe and welcoming environment for individuals to find strength, hope, and healing on their journey to recovery.

Alcoholics Anonymous (AA)
Website: www.aa.org
Alcoholics Anonymous was the first 12-step program, and it is the most well-known 12-step program. It provides support for individuals recovering from alcohol addiction.

Narcotics Anonymous (NA)
Website: www.na.org
Narcotics Anonymous offers support for individuals seeking recovery from drug addiction.

Cocaine Anonymous (CA)
Website: www.ca.org
Cocaine Anonymous is a fellowship for individuals recovering from cocaine addiction and other substance use disorders.

Al-Anon Family Groups
Website: www.al-anon.org
Al-Anon provides support to families and friends of individuals struggling with alcohol addiction.

Nar-Anon Family Groups
Website: www.nar-anon.org
Nar-Anon offers support to families and friends of individuals dealing with drug addiction.

Gamblers Anonymous (GA)
Website: www.gamblersanonymous.org
Gamblers Anonymous provides support to individuals recovering from gambling addiction.

Overeaters Anonymous (OA)
Website: www.oa.org
Overeaters Anonymous offers support for individuals struggling with compulsive overeating, binge eating, and other eating disorders.

Debtors Anonymous (DA)
Website: www.debtorsanonymous.org
Debtors Anonymous provides support to individuals dealing with financial challenges and compulsive spending.

Sex Addicts Anonymous (SAA)
Website: www.saa-recovery.org
Sex Addicts Anonymous offers support for individuals struggling with compulsive sexual behavior.

Emotions Anonymous (EA)
Website: www.emotionsanonymous.org
Emotions Anonymous is a fellowship for individuals dealing with emotional challenges and mood disorders.

Adult Children of Alcoholics (ACA)/Dysfunctional Families
Website: www.adultchildren.org
Adult Children of Alcoholics provides support for individuals who grew up in dysfunctional homes and struggle with the effects of childhood trauma.

———————

Please note that these programs follow a 12-step approach and are based on the principles of anonymity, fellowship, and personal responsibility. Each program operates independently and is self-supporting. If you are interested in joining a 12-step program, you can find local meetings and virtual resources through the respective websites. Remember, seeking help and support for addiction or behavioral challenges is a courageous step toward a healthier and more fulfilling life.

REFERENCES

Abraham, Micah. "How Anxiety Can Create Circulation Problems." *CalmClinic*. Updated October 10, 2020. https://www.calmclinic.com/anxiety/circulation-problems.

Aghajan, Zahra M., Peter Schuette, Tony A. Fields, Michelle E. Tran, Sameed M. Siddiqui, Nicholas R. Hasulak, Thomas K. Tcheng, et al. "Theta Oscillations in the Human Medial Temporal Lobe During Real-World Ambulatory Movement." *Current Biology* 27, no. 24 (2017): 3743–51. https://doi.org/10.1016/j.cub.2017.10.062.

Alshami, Ali M. "Pain: Is It All in the Brain or the Heart?" *Current Pain and Headache Reports* 23 (2019). https://doi.org/10.1007/s11916-019-0827-4.

Baric, Vedrana Bolic, Sofie Skuthälla, Malin Pettersson, Per A. Gustafsson, and Anette Kjellberg. "The Effectiveness of Weighted Blankets on Sleep and Everyday Activities: A Retrospective Follow-Up Study of Children and Adults with Attention Deficit Hyperactivity Disorder and/or Autism Spectrum

Disorder." *Scandinavian Journal of Occupational Therapy* (2021): 1–11. https://doi.org/10.1080/11038128.2021.1939414.

Chang, Anne-Marie, Daniel Aeschbach, Jeanne F. Duffy, and Charles A. Czeisler. "Evening Use of Light-Emitting eReaders Negatively Affects Sleep, Circadian Timing, and Next-Morning Alertness." *Proceedings of the National Academy of Sciences of the United States of America* 112, no. 4 (2015): 1232–37. https://doi.org/10.1073/pnas.1418490112.

Eron, Kathryn, Lindsey Kohnert, Ashlie Watters, Christina Logan, Melissa Weisner-Rose, and Philip S. Mehler. "Weighted Blanket Use: A Systematic Review." *American Journal of Occupational Therapy* 74, no. 2 (2020): 1–14. https://doi.org/10.5014/ajot.2020.037358.

Fanselow, Michael S. "Fear and Anxiety Take a Double Hit from Vagal Nerve Stimulation." *Biological Psychiatry* 73, no. 11 (2013). https://doi.org/10.1016/j.biopsych.2013.03.025.

Goldstein, Andrea N., and Matthew P. Walker. "The Role of Sleep in Emotional Brain Function." *Annual Review of Clinical Psychology* 10 (2014): 679–708. https://doi.org/10.1146/annurev-clinpsy-032813-153716.

Haynes, Trevor. "Dopamine, Smartphones & You: A Battle for Your Time." *Science in the News* (blog), May 1, 2018. https://sitn.hms.harvard.edu/flash/2018/dopamine-smartphones-battle-time.

König, Nicola, Sarah Steber, Josef Seebacher, Quinten von Prittwitz, Harald R. Bliem, and Sonja Rossi. "How Therapeutic Tapping Can Alter Neural Correlates of Emotional Prosody Processing in Anxiety." *Brain Sciences* 9, no. 8 (2019): 206. https://doi.org/10.3390/brainsci9080206.

Leproult, Rachel, Georges Copinschi, Orfeu Buxton, and Eve Van Cauter. "Sleep Loss Results in an Elevation of Cortisol Levels the Next Evening." *Sleep* 20, no. 10 (1997): 865–70.

Lovato, Nicole, and Leon Lack. "The Effects of Napping on Cognitive Functioning." *Progress in Brain Research* 185 (2010): 155–66. https://doi.org/10.1016/B978-0-444-53702-7.00009-9.

Noyed, Daniel. "Weighted Blanket Benefits." Sleep Foundation. Updated May 15, 2023. https://www.sleepfoundation.org /best-weighted-blankets/weighted-blanket-benefits.

Simon, Eti Ben, Aubrey Rossi, Allison G. Harvey, and Matthew P. Walker. "Overanxious and Underslept." *Nature Human Behavior* 4 (2020): 100–110. https://doi.org/10.1038/s41562 -019-0754-8.

Streeter, Chris C., Theodore H. Whitfield, Liz Owen, Tasha Rein, Surya K. Karri, Aleksandra Yakhkind, Ruth Perlmutter, Andrew Prescot, Perry F. Renshaw, Domenic A. Ciraulo, and J. Eric Jensen. "Effects of Yoga versus Walking on Mood, Anxiety, and Brain GABA Levels: A Randomized Controlled MRS Study." *The Journal of Alternative and Complementary Medicine* 16, no. 11 (Nov. 2010): 1145–52. https://doi.org /10.1089/acm.2010.0007.

To Write to the Author

If you wish to contact the author or would like more information about this book, please write to the author in care of Llewellyn Worldwide Ltd. and we will forward your request. Both the author and publisher appreciate hearing from you and learning of your enjoyment of this book and how it has helped you. Llewellyn Worldwide Ltd. cannot guarantee that every letter written to the author can be answered, but all will be forwarded. Please write to:

Amanda Huggins
⁒ Llewellyn Worldwide
2143 Wooddale Drive
Woodbury, MN 55125-2989

Please enclose a self-addressed stamped envelope for reply,
or $1.00 to cover costs. If outside the U.S.A., enclose
an international postal reply coupon.

Many of Llewellyn's authors have websites with additional information and resources. For more information, please visit our website at http://www.llewellyn.com.